Megan -
I can't even begin
to tell you how
incredibly happy I
am that we're
met. You're doing
incredible things -
and I can't wait
to watch it all
unfold.

I love you!

Jess

Please Validate My Existence

please validate my existence

essays & stories from a twentysomething pseudo-intellectual

Jessica Manuszak

Please Validate My Existence
by Jessica Manuszak

BOOK AND COVER DESIGN ©2015
BY Kevin Barrett Kane
thefrontispiece.com

THE FRONTISPIECE
BOULDER, CO

Dedication

This book is dedicated to you.
Yes, you. Stop looking behind you.
I mean you.

...and also probably David Hasselhoff, because
don't we all deserve a little recognition?

Table of Contents

Table of Contents

Table of Contents

Table of Contents

Welcome to ~~the jungle~~ this book.

(We've got fun & games. Also, bourbon.)

Fancy meeting you here!

(No, seriously. It's fancy. I'm even wearing pearls.)

CHANCES ARE, YOU'RE:

Someone who finds fart jokes funny. Who isn't ashamed of their midnight Taco Bell runs after inexplicably watching 7 back-to-back episodes of *Murder, She Wrote*. Who sings '90s rap songs in the shower and knows that every tea is better as an iced tea. You laugh, loudly and often. And most importantly? You're someone who's trying their best to adventure through this damn winding labyrinth* known as LIVING.

**David Bowie, sadly, is not included.*

THIS BOOK IS:

A bright little corner for the adventurers. The depressives. The occasional day drinkers. And anyone who knows they deserve just a little bit more. (And/or believes in *El Chupacabra.*)

Consider this a tasting menu of the most tantalizing essays I've ever penned, so you can wet your proverbial whistle and pick up a punch or two of inspiration along the way.

(I'd like to think of it as the equivalent of a drug dealer giving you just a little heroin. Y'know. Just so you can try it. And then come back for more over and over again until you find yourself celebrating your thirty-fifth birthday huddled in a soggy cardboard box and growling at your own feet whilst muttering deviantly about the government and painting on your face with the blood of a road-killed rabbit.)

Disclaimer: I DO NOT SELL HEROIN.

It's also worth noting that the most-used search term used to find me on the internet is consistently, "Jesus said, 'Why do you kick me in the gonads?'" If you're one of those people, I'm very sorry—I don't have an answer for you. But on the bright side? We have streamers here. Also, cake.

I hope you pick up what I'm about to put down. Pick it up, and give it a kiss, and tell it you love it so maybe you can get it into bed. Because if there's one thing you deserve, it's a steamy night in bed with a book. And this book? *Does all the weird stuff.*

Please Validate My Existence

1

On Animal Ass Juices

The year I turned thirteen, I spent the summer squeezing dogs' anal glands. For $6 an hour at the Wag 'n' Wash, I scraped soggy wads of animal hair out of a stainless steel sink, trying not to get bit by Raisin, a feisty black Bouvier with a deep, unrelenting hatred of people poking around his private poop hole. (I'm not blaming him, for the record.)

At fourteen, I was making pizza at a take-and-bake pizza joint by my high school. The older kids made out in the walk-in freezer against the piles of pepperoni, which couldn't have *possibly* been hygienic, and my very first "real" boyfriend broke up with me because my hands always smelled like pizza. (In other news, WHAT GUY DOESN'T WANT A GIRL WHO SMELLS LIKE PIZZA?!)

From years fifteen to twenty-two, I worked at a day camp for kids, getting paid to underage gamble at Chuck E. Cheese and color pictures of Rapunzel, wrapping up my days playing dodge ball and making magnets with Fuse Beads.

After that, shit went really downhill. Fresh off the farm and straight out of college, I accidentally ended up working as a telemarketer for a skeezy online university where I was selling $40,000 educations to people who couldn't afford to feed themselves, let alone fund a degree program that borderlines on being totally invalid.

Every time someone told me to fuck off I earned five points. Every time I got a death threat I earned fifteen. And every time I'd accumulated one hundred points, I treated myself to a manicure.

I was getting three manicures a week.

After I stormed out, the next year was a blur of bartending jobs where the sixteen year-old chef insisted on calling me *Sugartits*, a receptionist position at a fancypants design district where the coffee tables cost more than my yearly salary, a nannying gig with two-year old twins who liked to stuff the toes of my brand new black ballet flats with chewed up spaghetti, and a three-month stint where I earned my screw top wine money from writing the raunchiest erotica and self-publishing under a pen name on Amazon.

Eventually, my ass landed in a government finance job with a school district where I was a glorified secretary, eating dry, boiled chicken breast in the fluorescent cafeteria, and being reminded weekly that I needed to have less personality. That I needed to tone it down. That I needed to wear sensible flats and khaki slacks and imitation pearls.

I was being actively groomed to settle for mediocrity and resolve myself to a life of mundane meetings, which ultimately just made me want to stab myself in the left tit with a very large and rusty spork.

And that's when everything changed. I'd run the fucking gamut: scrubbed animal ass juice off my hands, tolerated sexual harassment, spritzed Febreeze on my wrinkled pants seven days running to try and cover up the weird vag smell that pants get when you wear them too many times in a row, and cried in my cubicle(s) more times than I can count on my fingers *and* my toes.

But while I didn't know exactly what I wanted, I knew exactly what I *didn't* want, and that's when things began to change.

Because of all my mistakes, meltdowns, and mess ups, I was able to hone in on what would make me happy and focus on what would make me feel fulfilled.

Cut to two years later. I've been on an all-expenses paid trip to Costa Rica for my career. I'm enthusiastically creeping up on my two-year anniversary with my dream company where I'm going to make a salary close enough to six figures that if I think too hard about it, I'm filled with such overwhelming gratitude that I feel the need to sob dramatically and throw myself onto a conveniently-placed nearby settee like a damn Disney princess. I'm disgustingly devoted and meaningfully motivated. And I could not possibly be more in love with what I do on the day-to-day.

So, that all being said?

You don't have to have all the answers.

You don't have to be 100% certain before surging forward.

If something sounds like a good idea, explore the hell out of it. If you hate it, it's another option you can eliminate. It's another item you can put in the *No Fucking Thank You* column. It's another shove in the right direction.

When you figure out what you don't want, you narrow in on what makes you tick, and that's what makes all the magic manifest.

(By "magic" I mean money, a bomb-ass career that leaves you feeling fucking fulfilled, and a future that makes you want to throw a party LL Cool J would be honored to attend.)

Put the pause on all the pressure to find the perfect profession.

Instead, get your feet wet, dive in dick-first, and don't allow yourself to apologize for enthusiastically adventuring through life. Your fulfillment will follow. You future will fall into place. And your happiness will happen.

And in the meantime? Go make a motherloving pizza. I hear it helps you date *all* the dudes.

2

On High-Anxiety Action Movies & Even Higher-Anxiety Boners

Decisions are like penises. (Sorry, mom).

They're supposed to be huge, hard, and ready to go at the drop of a hat.

But what happens when the choices you make aren't immediately life-changing? When your decisions are smaller, require preparation, and maybe won't change the course of your life instantly AND MAKE EVERYTHING SO MUCH DIFFERENT ALL THE TIME ALWAYS!?

Maybe you like your day job well enough. Chances are, you don't need to leave a big relationship. You're not interested in moving across the country, selling everything to travel, or cutting out an entire food group.

Yet you're still you, with a fire blazing in your belly and a light in your eyes.

In movies, there's always a get-it-together montage. It's jammed full of full-out sprints, bloody fights, ferocious packing, and character-building heartache. Big decisions. Big actions.

Screen shots are wide and encompassing, capturing the image that fists are clenched. Jaws are hard. Abs are sculpted.

The anticipation builds, stretching higher and higher towards that torturous crescendo, the defining moment finally breaking, leaving success and victory crashing down around the hero.

Audiences clap. Some might even cry. And if it's opening weekend, those people in the front few rows with neck aches probably stand and holler, because after witnessing change like *that*, there's just no going back.

And then there's me. Sitting at my computer in my little sun-soaked apartment, typing away contentedly and talking about my vagina too much on the internet. Sometimes I pause for a while, sipping on green tea that's mostly just water with liberal squirts of honey and thinking that I should pluck my eyebrows, or at the very least, the little sprouts of creep-ass hairs that grow out of my chin.

My foot bobbles around. I take ~~breaks~~ distinguished constitutionals and stroll around the block. Usually there's not even music playing, and OH MY GOD, HOW CAN LIFE CHANGES HAPPEN WITHOUT WICKED SWEET BASS BEATS?!

Slowly. Steadily.

And persistently.

That's how.

While it's absolutely true that huge change often equates to personal growth, that isn't to say that personal growth only comes from huge change. Sure, everyone loves the gut-twisting drama of a good turning point (myself included).

Sometimes those tough actions have to happen.

And I promise you that if and when those times come, I'll be the first to tie my hair back and sprint up some stairs, slap those street-wise mob guys around and move to a tiny Irish town, probably avenging the death of someone named Javier and hopefully looking great while battling intense mental anguish coupled with unwavering determination and a sky-high pair of red heels.

But you don't have to wait for that big life-changing pivotal moment to make shit happen, because opportunities for growth *surround you all the time.*

Reading an extra two pages on marketing before bed, or complimenting someone in the supermarket, or organizing your kitchen cupboards are all getting you closer to being the person you know you want to be. Hell, even getting chatty with your barista in the morning has a measurable (positive) impact on your mood all day.

It might not be as glamorous. It might not make for an action-packed film. And it might not be as immediately gratifying.

But that sure as hell doesn't mean those quiet opportunities for growth aren't *just* as fucking important.

3

On What You Were "Born" to Be

(besides a weird, flaky baby who would later shove a jumbo crayon up your sose, only to have emergency surgery to remove the damn thing)

I'm tired of guided meditations. I'm tired of needing to connect with some fuzzy wuzzy higher power who's going to *enlighten* me about my *divine purpose*. And I'm tired of feeling this insane pressure to choose only ONE path because we each have ONE true version of ourselves, that apparently is so lost it constantly needs finding.

When did life become more about committing to our destinies and less about "choose your own adventure" books?

In case you've forgotten, life isn't about finding yourself. It's about creating yourself, about intentionally cultivating, sculpting, and inventing the most impressive, astounding, sexy version of you that is humanly possible.

So you want to be a marathon runner? Run marathons. So you

want to be a novelist? Write novels. So you want be a veterinarian? ~~Cut open your cat.~~ Go to vet school.

There is nothing stopping you, other than these preconceived notions you have of yourself in that squishy little brain of yours.

The truth of the matter is that the world can change.

People can change. *You* can change. The only reason we fall back on who we've always been is because it's who we've always been, creating a self-perpetuating cycle of sameness. BREAK THE CYCLE.

The past doesn't automatically determine your future, but the choices you make in the present sure as hell do.

So please, take responsibility for your decisions. Care about those decisions. And most importantly, stop being such a discouraging dick to yourself about making those decisions in the first place. ALL THE NICE FOREVER AND EVER, *capisce?*

At the end of it all, I just need you to know that no one is born to be anything other than completely and entirely impressive.

4

On Enthusiastically Choking People To Death

We're supposed to go the gym every morning, halfheartedly pedaling on an elliptical while listening to the same mind-numbing chart topper call us *baby* just one too many times.

Showered and dressed, we hop on our computer, check the hundreds of emails and simultaneously text, all while drinking coffee that's turned lukewarm over the course of the morning.

It's required that we spend some time first researching recipes, then ultimately wandering through the too-big store packed with strangers, setting ingredients in the cart, finally stir-frying 100% organic vegetables, (no meat, no sodium, no sugar) for a dinner that we eat in silence.

We're told to pursue hobbies. Knit scarves and go jogging, collect old pennies and alphabetize our movie collection.

Straighten our Pottery Barn® decorative pillows on our couch each time we stand up. Unload the dishwasher so the spoons face the same way in the drawers. Check our emails again.

And don't forget that it's important to find time to wash our delicates on the lowest spin cycle so we *never* have to resort to donning those outdated bikini bottoms that seem to always smell like chlorine no matter how many times you wash them.

After a day of working 12 hours (to impress our bosses), we come home, and it's time to settle in and read some fiction, and then some non-fiction, preferably at a 1:1 ratio. Iron our shirts. Meditate. Journal for an hour and really contemplate our day, all while perfectly managing social media accounts, packing a salad of baby greens for our next day full of kitten heels and acidic decaf (two Splendas), then changing into pristine, lacy lingerie and initiating tender (yet satisfying) sex with our partners.

And by integrating all of these time-consuming, moving parts into our precious 24-hour segments, we're letting it all merge together into a harmonious soup of life fulfillment, right? (Think less *Hungry Man* stew and more Whole Foods lobster bisque.)

The bottom line is that we try to be stable. We want to be balanced. We all strive to be well-rounded.

And it's time we knock it off.

Because I don't know about you, but even writing those two paragraphs was exhausting. I literally feel overwhelmed right now just thinking about trying to divide my time into all of that shit I don't care about when all I want to do is go to my hour-long cycling class and then have a beer or three with lunch.

But stress barfs aside, the important bit is that when you do everything, you accomplish nothing.

See also: WHEN YOU'RE MEDIOCRE AT EVERYTHING, YOU'RE EXCEPTIONAL AT NOTHING. And before you have time to fold another pair of stupid slacks or watch a mindless sitcom, you've found yourself filling the role of another faceless nobody just trying to find the balance.

But you?

You deserve to BE SOMEBODY.

You deserve to invest in yourself, figuring out your passion and fighting your way to a place of perfection, whatever that means to you. You deserve to burn that half-finished scarf, put down the damn crossword (unless you actually love doing the crossword), and bid your balance *adieu*.

And you deserve to take that energy you're unceremoniously chucking into handfuls of *supposed to*s and *should*s and aggressively shove it into whatever it is that puts the swagger in your step and the rhythm in your rest.

Be relentless about what you love. Resolve to be remarkable. And decide to dedicate your time towards something that actually matters.

But most of all?

Stop trying to be well-rounded.

Instead, strive to be spiky, so the world has no choice but to fucking choke on you.

5

On All Of The Adages You Need To Ignore, Cockblock & Banish From Existence

1. There's no place like home.

Uh. Have you ever been to Disney Land? Because that place is pretty sweet.

But while "home" is safe and comforting and welcoming, don't be afraid to find other new places that fit the bill. Maybe there's a cafe in Paris that gives you all the same warm fuzzies, or an acquaintance's SoHo loft that smells just like your mom. (Let's pretend that's not as weird as it sounds.)

It's great that your home is a haven, just don't use that as an excuse to stay put forever.

You might have roots, but you're not a tree, and it's time to go exploring.

2. Love is never having to say you're sorry.

Look. Relationships are hard, and you're going to screw up. A lot. And if you don't apologize, you'll be kicked to the curb, (and possibly in the groin), faster than you can say, "Pickleball." (I don't actually know what that is, but my gym offers classes. It also has a "wet craft" room. I've decided not to inquire.)

3. You can't judge a book by its cover.

What?! OF COURSE YOU CAN.

Have you ever seen a Nicholas Sparks cover? (In case you haven't, let's all take a moment to appreciate that they're all white people almost kissing.)

And while they might not be the most inventive covers, they tell you immediately what's inside. People judge books by their covers all the time, (both literally and figuratively), so GET YOURSELF A DAMN GOOD COVER. (P.S. This is where I hug the everloving hell out of The Frontispiece for designing this book and making me look like a damn pro when mostly I just talk about bodily excretions.)

4. All that glitters isn't gold.

Yeah, because some of it's silver. Or copper. Or that fake glitter they put on cupcakes. *Mmm,* cupcakes.

This goes along with, "If it sounds too good to be true, it probably is," to which I say, EXCEPT FOR WHEN IT ISN'T.

Good things exist. *Great* things exist. And I promise you can have them. (And I'm not even crossing my fingers behind my back.)

5. Keep your friends close and your enemies closer.

Keep your friends close and then AVOID ENEMIES ALWAYS.

Because becoming bosom buddies with your nemesis almost always leads to stabbing, or at the very least, some pretty passive aggressive Facebook posts. (And don't even get me started on the phrase *bosom buddies*. NO ONE GETS TO BE FRIENDS WITH MY BOOBS UNLESS I SAY SO.)

6. If you can't beat 'em, join 'em.

No. Always beat them. Preferably with a very large stick.

7. Curiosity killed the cat.

Curiosity didn't kill the cat. Curiosity made the cat better at cooking souffles, experienced in all things fellatio, and *way* better at pool.

Wonder about everything. Learn about anything you can get your hands on. And be so much better for it. (Bonus: You can feel smug as fuck when you know more answers than your friends whilst watching *Jeopardy*.)

8. Absence makes the heart grow fonder.

...But also paranoid, distant, inexplicably jealous, and pissy.

Because at its finest, absence actually makes the heart fight with the other heart over the phone and sometimes via Skype and then eat peanut butter off a spoon while silently weeping over an episode of *Golden Girls*. (Don't say I didn't warn you.)

9. All good things come to those who wait.

You know what comes to those who wait? Nothing. Except really long hair, because growing it out long enough to have a casual, wavy French braid takes *so* much time.

In reality, all good things come to those who go out and *make* them happen. And don't you forget it.

10. A bird in the hand is worth two in the bush.

[INSERT LOW-BROW PUBIC HAIR JOKE HERE.]

6

On Thongs

Hypothetically, say this last Tuesday found you wearing roughly 70 bajillion layers, sitting in front of the panda habitat at the Denver Zoo, and alternating between licking a soft-serve ice cream cone (chocolate and vanilla swirl), and wiping snot on your new chartreuse chevron scarf.

Hypothetically, say you spent five hours at this zoo, alone, looking into the mostly-empty enclosures and sitting on your hands to make sure they didn't fall off from frostbite (which would be highly unlikely, but not impossible), trying to smile politely at the other people who were at the zoo in the middle of the day during the (most) dead of winter, and wishing a stranger would come up and start a movie-worthy conversation.

"You okay, Love?" they'd ask.

And you'd smile in a way that made you somehow both charming and vulnerable.

Then you'd probably fall in love with the stranger and get married and also find pirate treasure and live in a giant tree house like the Swiss Family Robinson, except instead of kids you'd just adopt too many turtles and spend a lot of time tanning and eating chocolate truffles off of Brad Pitt's sculpted abs like some people eat sushi off of nude models.

But I digress.

And hypothetically, let's say your best friend of 7 years got your text that was just one of those slanty-faced emoticons that manage to convey more about apathy and stress and struggle than a whole slew of expletives, took the afternoon off work, and found you with the gorillas, your right palm pressed melodramatically against the glass as you watched the big one (who weirdly reminded you of your grandpa), picking fruit slices out of a giant plastic ball.

:-/

And then, let's say, you got all weepy. Because fighting for what you want all the time can be exhausting. Because sometimes you feel like everyone is doing better than you—doing more than you, every second of every day, and you're behind the fucking 8 ball like Indiana Jones, streaking through your to-do list but never eliminating that crushing sense of needing to *do more*.

Play bigger. Get better.

Those feelings, those urges, to build and grow and improve and thrive, are what set your eyes alight. Those urges are what encourage you to try harder, work smarter, *blah blah blah.*

But they're also what make you get nose goop all over the collar of your peacoat while openly crying in public, rambling about every stress that has ever existed in the history of the mother-loving world, only taking time to gulp big breaths of air in order to continue the tirade about people getting sick and deadlines looming and projects bubbling and momentum building and giraffe's being, like, *gulp of air* such beautiful, *beautiful* creatures.

And that's when your hypothetical friend who is a hypothetical manager for a high-end lingerie company leans over the railing, takes a big whiff of the giraffe stench, and says, "Look. At the end of the day, it's all just bras and panties."

It's all just bras and panties.

It's all just little details. It's all just white noise. It's all just clutter that distracts you from living.

Your shoulders relaxed, and then it was just the two of you, looking at the dead grass as women with strollers full of babies strolled by, (and you totally realized that's probably why they're called strollers), the only sounds coming from the sloppy chewing of the giraffe with his huge purple tongue and your sporadic sniffles.

The stress. The overwhelm. The emails. The ideas. The sleepless nights. The personal bullshit. The things that feel like

OH, SWEET JESUS, THIS IS THE ACTUAL END, are just little details.

So, hypothetically, next time you want to crawl into a cave somewhere in New Zealand, pull a rock over the opening and cram fistfuls of marshmallows into your face, just remember to take things a little less seriously. To breathe just a little bit deeper. And remember that at the end of the day...

It's all just little scraps of lace that go up your buttcrack.

7

On The Gates To Hell...Or At Least Mindless Mediocrity

There are three things I know to be true:

1) Some things actually taste as good as being thin feels. (I'm lookin' at you, mango habanero hot wings.)

2) Before I had my tonsils out, I always sneezed in perfect sets of three, and now I only sneeze in twos. This is likely a government conspiracy.

3) *Torschlusspanik* is a very real, and very daunting feeling—not to mention a thick mouthful of German.

Torschlusspanik (n.): The fear, usually as one gets older, that time is running out and important opportunities are slipping away.

Actually, if you translate it directly, you wind up with "gate shut panic"—that adrenalizing feeling of new experiences slamming their rattling windows shut in your face as minutes, hours, months, years tick right on by. And no one is immune to *Torschlusspanik's* evil charms.

Because no matter how focused you are on the end game, there will always be those what-ifs hanging in the air like fireflies and tempting you with their painfully whimsical winking lights to take a closer look. To imagine a different life where you moved to a quaint mountain town instead of the big city. To dip the tip of your pinky finger into the reality where you became an online entrepreneur instead of an elementary school teacher.

But does something as trivial as the hand on a clock or pages being ripped from a Dilbert desk calendar actually have the authority to padlock our courage in cages, slam all the mahogany doors to our ideal images of success, and prevent us from packing up our kitchens and moving to that quaint mountain town?

Ah, hell naw.

Yet that doesn't change the fact that we're scared of numbers. The numbers in our bank accounts, the numbers on the office clock, the number of years we have left.

We hunker down in security, pulling our duvets over our under-slept heads and vowing that maybe we'll give our what-if wonderings a try in the month of Nevuary, watching the hourglass run out of sand.

And that's the most important reason to pry open all those "closed" opportunities with a crowbar—to put our backs into it and let the sweat trace lines down our spines.

A reason to wrap our hands in dish towels, tightening our palms into fists and smash those pristine glass boxes so pompously reserved in case of emergency.

A reason to get your boots dirty and kick down those doors that feel so set on creaking shut, fighting to get our grubby little hands on the great lives we know we want.

Time is constantly leaking through our outstretched fingers, dripping onto the pavement and challenging us to do something significant with the amount of it we have left.

But the gates don't close unless we let them.

Because time is just a set of nothing numbers, little hash marks on a wall letting us know that our planet has made another rotation. But your life? Your life is worth every single second of struggle, every rounded drop of determination, and every final moment of fight.

8

On Growing An Impressive, Hairy Pair Of Gonads That Flap About Merrily In The Summer Breeze

Find your voice. Shout into a pillow until your voice is gravelly and sultry. Yell from an open window and startle innocent passersby. Sing too loudly to a song on the freeway, and remind yourself that you deserve to be heard.

Stop saying you're lucky. You are not lucky, you are accomplished. You are proud. You are hard-working, and the positive things you have, you have because you've earned them. Unless the positive thing you have is a positive STD test, in which case, *daaaaaaaaaang.*

Decide. Choose which path you're going to start forging, hacking through the bullshit and making your own way. And then do it. Because nothing noteworthy ever happens from living at a crossroads except watching people botch four-way stops. ("No, you go." "No, *you* go." "IT WAS MY TURN!")

Remember that you are not less than or equal to. You are greater. Greater than settling. Greater than mediocrity. Greater than living inside a tight little box and gazing wistfully out into the big, wide world. You are a force of nature, like a damn hurricane that tears shutters off windows and shit (but doesn't leave anyone homeless. That's not cool, you guys.)

Quit waiting for your hero. Quit waiting for some magic solution to appear. Quit waiting for your boat to come in. You've got to dive in and swim out to meet it, otherwise you'll be stranded on a desert island, sunburned and without any rum. The worst part? Johnny Depp won't even be there with you.

Explore. The world. Your body. Your neighbor's body. New cheeses. Fast music. Old cars. And that cave entrance you have to take a boat to that everyone says is haunted. (Bring talismans. And maybe a machete.)

Eat cake. Eat cake with your hands, and drink scotch out of the bottle, and take long bike rides during that perfect time when the sun is rising and the world is cool and quiet. Because life is short. Because scotch is delicious. Because why wouldn't you?

Do THAT thing. That big thing that you've been putting off. Shaving words into the back of your head. Moving cities so you can start auditioning for Broadway musicals while wearing leotards. Ending a bad relationship that started on Tinder and should have stayed there. Illegally adopting a penguin that you will promptly name Sir Francis. The *right time* doesn't exist, so just *make* time.

Don't stop. You're going to want to quit. You're going to want to stop writing. Stop running. Stop cooking. Stop believing. Don't. Because how are you ever going to succeed if you stop trying? Failure isn't permanent.* Giving up is.

**And face tattoos. Face tattoos are also permanent.*

Pinpoint what it is that totally gets you off, and do more of it.

No excuses.

9

On Being The Ugliest Motherfucker Who Builds Blanket Forts

Three years ago, when I was fresh out of ~~Compton~~ college, I was riding the bus to work, a free commuter shuttle that shuffled my kitten-heeled heiny to the tallest building in downtown Denver where I'd accidentally become a telemarketer for $18.75 an hour. (I stayed there for quite awhile, despite crying into three gin and tonics nearly every night after work. This is referred to as the "golden handcuffs," ladies and gents.)

But as I stood there with my hand clutching the metal pole caked with the greyish grime that only comes from thousands of peoples' palms, I stared into the nothingness as I prepared myself for another day of hundreds of cold calls to people who would either a) hang up on me, b) threaten to murder me or c) threaten to murder both me and my family.

A woman sitting on one of the faded orange bench cushions

stained with something that looked a lot like piss looked up at me with her brow furrowed, her cheeks filling with air as her hands clenched.

I watched her watch me in the same way you watch commercials on TV; mindless engagement with an unintentional layer of disinterest. Her cheeks bowing out to maximum capacity, she finally exploded. "YOU ARE SO UGLY." I blinked back at her blankly, completely unsure of what to do, and she continued to shout it over and over, spit pooling in the chapped corners of her mouth while her fists pummeled the tops of her thighs.

"YOU ARE SO UGLY."

"YOU ARE SO UGLY."

"YOU'RE THE UGLIEST MOTHERFUCKER I'VE EVER SEEN."

The packed bus stared at me and the floor while I stared first at the woman, and then at the bus driver, and then at the floor. A renegade cherry-flavored chapstick rolled across the sticky black floor mat, and I watched it disappear under a seat. No one said anything while the record of this woman screaming was stuck on repeat, her voice growing louder and more graveled.

At the next stop, I politely muttered my way through the throngs and stepped out onto the concrete. The woman followed, and as I literally sprinted the five remaining blocks to the building that would calm me with its marble floors and carpeted cubicle walls, she ran just as quickly, continuing her insult on loop.

Finally, I shoved my way through the glass revolving doors and stopped to catch my breath, turning around to see her sweaty and disheveled, visibly vibrating with rage.

"YOU," she yelled, jabbing her finger into the pane of glass that separated us, "YOU DON'T DESERVE TO BE ALIVE, YOU'RE SO UGLY."

She left a smudge on the window with the oil from her hands, her nose pressing against the glass while her spit made rivulets down the wall. Eventually, a bird caught her eye, and she wandered slowly back the way she'd came, muttering under her breath and adjusting the plastic grocery bags she had wrapped around her feet.

The front desk security guard strode over, placed his hand on my shoulder and asked if I was alright. I mumbled, *Fine.* I mumbled, *Of course.*

I walked promptly into the stairwell, resolutely trudging up all 17 flights, counting my breaths as I sobbed hysterically, dabbing at my wing-tipped eyeliner while my hands shook violently of their own volition.

The world can be an ugly, hateful place.

It can shove you down, spit on your stomach, and then walk away unscathed, leaving you curled on the concrete and wishing for rain. It can strip you of your sincerity and violate your vulnerability. It can make you doubt yourself, your future, your entire life—regardless of the fact that it could have been you on that bus or someone who looked nothing like you, just a filler for unintentional hurt from a stranger.

But while it can sometimes seem like there's poison seeping into unswept corners and venom finding home in hearts & heads, there's also unlimited amounts of beauty. Unabashed bounties of hope. And bottomless wells of well-wishes.

Now, this isn't where I blow a perfectly-scented puff of Chanel No. 5 up your asshole and tell you everything's going to be fine if you stop and smell the roses.

This?

This is where I beg you to build a blanket fort in your living room, camping out on a Monday night in front of the air conditioning and falling asleep to the soothing voices of NPR's *This American Life*.

This is where I urge you to slip through the gap in your sliding glass door and let your fingers memorize the veins of the largest leaf on your blooming and unruly poplar tree.

And this is where I dare you to take out a pumpkin spice candle smack dab in the middle of the raging July heat—the only candle you have in your entire apartment—and huddle in the fort, lighting the wick and letting it simmer, clenching your eyes closed and wishing hard. For you. For your future. For your entire life.

That same life that can seem shrouded in hateful shit, but is actually magnetic in its magnificence and oh-so-wonderfully whimsical. And blowing out that tiny flame with a slightly larger puff of air from those lungs that dully glowed while carrying you up those 17 flights of stairs, remember what it means to let the magic make a home in your curved and cupped hands.

To exhale until your ribs fold in on themselves, relieved with the relaxation. To lay beneath a blanket, the extinguished smoke slightly stinging your nostrils and making you more sure than ever that every single thing is going to be okay.

10

On Making Everyone Hate Your Guts

1. When a coworker approaches and offers up the standard, "Oh! You got a haircut!" reply simply with, "Actually, I got all of them cut. Not just one."

2. When a new friend invites you over for dinner, ask to use the bathroom, and then go into their closet and shit in their shoes. (Easy, right?)

3. Anytime anyone, anywhere asks what time it is, respond that it's time for them to get a watch.

4. Make sure to say, "That's what she said!" in response to any conversation, especially when it doesn't make any sense and/or you're having dinner with your Nana.

5. If a colleague approaches you, shouting about some missed

deadline and waving around paperwork you literally could not care less about, you should probably inform them that you'd love to address their concerns, but you can't hear them over their obnoxiously loud blouse and/or tie.

6. When the overwhelmed guy at Starbucks accidentally forgets to put in your extra shot of espresso or heat the milk to your perfect temperate for your latte, be sure to tear everyone in the near vicinity a bloody new asshole before finally declaring that young people these days just don't have any personal integrity.

7. Speak only in rhymes for an entire day. Bonus points if you have jury duty.

8. Next time you're in K-Mart, take a sandwich out of the deli, eat half, and then stuff the rest into a boot over in the shoe section. Be sure to leave a note inside with your Twitter handle so the employee can later show you their appreciation.

9. When walking on a crowded sidewalk and maneuvering through throngs of busy people, stop abruptly and often.

10. Next time you're on the bus, sneeze into your hand and then wipe it on the seat.

11. If you send an email to a business at 9:00 p.m. on a Friday night, follow up again at 9:30, and then at 10:01, and then at 8:22 the next morning, (etc.) letting the emails escalate until you're drunk off boxed wine Sunday night and typing in all caps, threatening to call your lawyer and confessing that you'll never love again.

12. When eating dinner at a restaurant, be sure to order the soup and swish it audibly around in your mouth before swallowing loudly, belching, and proclaiming, “Oh, yeah. That’s the stuff.”

13. On Facebook, only post about terrible, heart-wrenching causes that are always certifiable scams. Also, get into lots of fights about politics and religion whenever anyone posts anything.

14. When you find yourself on a crowded elevator with your sexual partner, be sure to call each other, “baby” and “honeypot” as often as possible, openly caressing each other’s genitalia on the ride.

15. Next time you give a speech, ask the audience repeatedly if they’re excited, and then insist you can’t hear them. “Are you excited? I can’t hear you! I said, ‘Are you EXCITED?!’” Continue until people begin sneaking out the back.

16. When a blind date is excitedly telling you about how they had the absolute funnest time in Paris last year, run your finger around the rim of your wine glass and say, “That’s so cool! I’ve never had the *funnest* time in Paris, but once I did have the *most fun* time.” And then shit in their shoes.

17. Get your own face tattooed on your bicep.

18. Have one of those voicemail greetings that goes, “Hey! ... How are you? ...Oh, really? ....Cool! ....Gotcha! This is actually my message machine!”

19. Still refer to your voicemail as a message machine in daily conversation.

20. At least three times a day, bombard all of your social networking profiles with photos of the healthy, vegan, vegetarian, gluten-free, sugar-free, guilt-free soup you made that looks like corn diarrhea.

21. When having a fight with your significant other, scream, "I KNOW YOU ARE, BUT WHAT AM I?!" repeatedly until the neighbor below you bangs on their ceiling with a Swiffer Wet Jet.

22. Be that neighbor who bangs on their ceiling with a Swiffer Wet Jet.

23. When standing in a really long line with lots of other people standing in the long line, be the one who crosses their arms and sighs loudly every 7.4 seconds, rolling your eyes so hard the room starts to spin

24. Every time you're at the gym, do that weight machine where you squeeze your thighs together, and make really aggressive eye contact with anyone who will look at you.

25. Reveal too much about your personal life (including your gallstones, bunions, and inability to find a proper mating partner for your cat) to customer service personnel, such as the girl at your apartment front desk or the cashier at the grocery store.

26. As often as possible, tell anyone who will listen how you just "forget to eat" and "just can't stop losing weight."

27. Promise a new sex pal risque pictures, but then repeatedly

only send photos of your hairy, 76 year-old neighbor mowing his lawn.

28. If you live in a crowded apartment complex, take up the electric guitar, and practice just enough that everyone knows about your new hobby, but not so often that you actually get any good. (Pro tip: 1:38 a.m. on a Monday morning is prime time to pluck those ol' guitar strings.)

29. When you make toast, make sure to get as many toast crumbs into the butter container, and butter in the jelly jar. Clean condiments are overrated.

30. Say the words corn diarrhea, genitalia, snot, and bunions in the same essay and then just SHIT IN EVERYONE'S SHOES.

11

On Getting Too ~~Sexually~~ Excited

Sometimes, I like to act like I'm a functioning member of society, put on ~~pants~~ leggings, and sometimes even lipstick, posting up at a Starbucks and trying to look regal.

Occasionally, I'll even mutter under my breath while I look over my day planner so I can pretend like I'm a real life grown up who has agendas and 401k's and things, despite the fact that I probably just horked down a handful of stale Wheat Thins for breakfast.

And this morning while I chugged my iced chai, there was a group of high school girls squealing over a text from a guy named Johnny, holding each other's hands and literally jumping up and down from pure, uninhibited happiness.

The woman next to me glanced at the girls, rolled her eyes, made a giant huffy noise, (not to be confused with a huffing noise), and glanced over at me, leaning in and muttering a conspiratorial, "Can you *belieeeeeeeeve* them?"

And as I looked at this woman's wrinkled nose and disapproving stare, it hit me.

Somewhere down the line, we start believing that it's unacceptable to be excited.

That it's uncool to be uncollected.

That perfect moments are like, *so* passé.

And that a group of girls, boisterously bubbling with life, are worthy of disdain.

So. This is where I backhand you, shaking your shoulders just a little too roughly and shouting, "GET IT TOGETHER, MAN!" because I just can't seem to help myself.

Because it's time to get excited.

To get too excited.

To get ALL THE EXCITED. About anything. About everything. About nothing at all.

To throw literal, heaping handfuls of confetti on your birthday. To yell at the screen in movie theaters. (Bonus points if it includes the phrase, "DON'T OPEN THAT DOOR!") To cry from complete, overwhelming elation when the next book in a series comes out.

Stop underplaying how absolutely incredible the world is and start riotously celebrating your life.

Because in case you haven't noticed, *you only get one.*

12

On Popping Your Head Off & Pouring In The Piping Hot Warm & Fuzzies

You're going to reach a point when you've had enough. When your fire is muted, each small coal having abandoned its orange glow, settling into the sea of dark gray matter. At some point, your fight will leave you. You'll wrap your arms around your knees and hug so tightly, holding yourself together when you so desperately want to fall apart.

There's going to be a time when you unravel, come apart at the seams, and puddle loosely on the hardwood floor that hasn't been swept since St. Patrick's Day of last year.

There's going to be a time when you feel like you're not doing your best work. When you feel like you're not being your best self. When you sit in the silence and think about what can change, picking at your cuticles and feeling like you're wasting time.

Contemplating an early wake up time, more space for dreaming, more movement, and more blissful mess before shaking your head and shuttering the windows.

There's going to be a time when you can't sleep. When each second that passes just drives home that YOU. ARE NOT. AT PEACE. Tossing and turning and doubting and loathing. Times when you sleep too much—your legs too heavy and your brain too battered from the sheer exhaustion of always running from who you're terrified of becoming.

There's going to be a time when you fall in love, quickly and without reservation, just as there will be a time when you fall out of love just as harshly, the reality smacking you in the nose as you stare across the table at the person you once thought you'd be with forever and realize you no longer want to brush your fingers over the freckles on their shoulders, that you no longer want to combine the heat of your body with the heat of their body, that you no longer like their company.

There's going to be a time when you just want to rest. Crawl into a dark, warm cocoon and rest your weary bones until the soul sickness subsides. Until you can, once again, pull yourself up by the proverbial bootstraps and take one more step forward. (Because after all, a tiny step forward is still a step forward.)

There's going to be a time when you compare yourself to others. To the woman standing in front of you in line, effortlessly poised in her nude heels. To the runner who's 20 yards ahead of you during each and every race. To your Facebook friend from high school who you haven't spoken to in years, but is now (seemingly) happily married with two kids, even though they sometimes post racist articles and you're not even sure you want to share a beer with them—let alone share their life.

There's going to be a time when you want to give up. On your 5K. On your relationship. On your life.

And while it's okay to stumble, stutter over declarations and temporarily lose your way, know this:

There's going to be a time when you realize that all the things that have made your insides ache in that deep, hollow chamber somewhere between your ribs, are the same things that have been the most transformative. That have helped you define yourself. That have shown you what you're capable of going through and coming out the other side better off.

There's going to be a time when only you know what's best for you. When no amount of advice or research or psychic readings or wishing and wishing and wishing into your fisted hands during the dead of night can guide you as well as your gut.

There's going to be a time when you look back on all the other times and feel the nostalgia settle in your stomach for the days your insomnia granted you late-night trips to dimly-lit diners. A time when you let go of the anger and bitterness and disappointment and sadness, releasing it into the wind and watching it dissolve like all things dissolve–slowly, and completely.

I know it can be hard to remember how brilliant you are. How your smile is unlike anyone else's smile in the whole entire world. How you are an important and non-negotiable part of this large and stunning universe. How your eyelashes so perfectly catch your sweat. The way the hairs on your arms stand up in a standing ovation when the saxophonist on the corner hits the perfect note.

But when the path seems dark, and lonely, and likely riddled with murderers and/or pillaging pirates, remember these words.

Remember the way it feels to blow out birthday candles, the gentle puff of your breath holding the power to change the world. Remember the way your muscles melt after a late summer hike. Remember that you are strong. And you are capable. And you are whole.

You are enough, regardless of where you've been or where you plan on going.

And I am so very, very proud of you. For being here. For sticking around. And for trying, every single day.

13

On Telling Success to Suck A Shlong (Suck-sess?)

My seventh birthday found me sitting squarely in the principal's office, tennis shoes *thunk-thunk-thunking* on the front of his desk that I now know came from a mail order catalog, but at the time, was convinced had been carved by a blind artisan and imported from somewhere in Italy.

Long story less long, I'd tackled a boy on the playground, punched him square in the arm and then ran away and cried incoherent, snotty tears in the tire swing. He'd made fun of my favorite sweater, a knee-length beauty that was fuchsia with lime green trim—though what really made it special were the crocheted flowers that literally hung down on 3-inch strings of yarn around the bottom.

It was a weird choice for seven year-old Jessica, (the sweater, not the punching), but when I saw it for $0.75 at Goodwill, I knew I had to have it. So twice a week, I'd wake up twenty minutes early, take my flower sweater out of the dryer, and spend an episode of Power Rangers delicately untangling the dangling adornments.

And no one—NO ONE—was going to ridicule my favorite clothing choice.

But sitting in that principal's office, watching the back of my shoes light up with each kick and staring very intently at the freckle on my pointer finger, I was waiting for my parents to come pick me up, whisk me home, and lock me away forever in a tower (not unlike Rapunzel) as punishment.

The time ticked and tocked on by, and finally the principal looked up from the stack of papers he'd been shuffling and reshuffling, cleared the layer of settled phlegm out of his throat by taking a sip of his lukewarm coffee that was nearly white from so much powdered creamer, and leaned back in his plastic desk chair.

"You have a bright future in front of you," he said. "You know that, right?"

"I guess," I mumbled noncommittally.

He steepled his fingers, and I tried not to stare at the unsettling yellowed bed of his fingernails.

"You can be anything you want to be when you grow up. But not if you keep punching kids."

This was a legitimate point, and I shrugged, fingering the fray of the ugliest and most worn flower on my sweater.

"What do you want be?" he asked, his eyebrows raised pleasantly.

And I looked up just long enough to stare into his watery blue eyes, clasp my seven year-old hands in my seven year-old lap, and say clearly:

"Impressive."

Because success to me has always looked like perfectly-tailored skirt suits. It has looked like embossed business cards in a slim metal case, an office with floor-to-ceiling windows, and a large desk that comes from a mail order catalog, but gives kids the impression it was hand carved by a blind artisan and shipped from somewhere in Italy.

Success has been stilettos that click resolutely on linoleum floors, Skinny Double Shot Sugar-Free Vanilla Lattes delivered by an assistant, and conferences in Milwaukee. Interoffice gossip and sex in the fluorescent-lit copy room. I wanted an engraved nameplate hanging outside my closeable door.

Because success, for me, has always been more about how I look, and less about how I feel. More about how I seem, and less about how I'm succeeding. More about the words on a resume and less about the reality of the world.

I had my "real" success. It meant being micromanaged. It meant a sweaty boss telling me my heels made my ass look nice. It meant spreadsheets, and always being too busy, too tired, too mind-numbingly overworked to do anything other than hit the drive-through on the way home, eating a drooping burger on my couch while zoning out during a commercial for whatever prescription promised me I could run through fields of wildflowers and have a puppy if only I'd take their pill.

And I was miserable.

But changing careers, packing up my corner office into an embarrassingly small cardboard box with rips in the corners and taking the commuter train home for the very last time was terrifying. Not because I was losing health insurance, or my 401k, or paid vacations.

But because I had to redefine what success meant.

Because I had to admit that I'd been wrong—dead wrong for *decades.*

Because I had to rebuild my reality.

Ultimately, I found my answer in Richard Feynman, a longtime idol of mine who is my new complete epitome of success. Known for his work in theoretical physics (& for being an excellent bongo player), what makes Richard Feynman so important at the end of the day?

He's someone I want to know.

And that's a much better measure of personal achievement than business cards and artfully-coiled chignons.

Simply put, success means living a life that's shaping you into someone you'd want to buy a round of expensive scotch.

As for me? Today I woke with the sun. I ate a snack-sized candy bar before walking along the river and listening to the footfall of runners padding rhythmically by. I showered, dressed for the day in underwear and a tank top, and sat cross-legged on the couch. And with both the curtains and my laptop wide open to the world, I started my work day the same I start all my new work days: by diving in to the projects that matter most to me. It's officially been a year since I left "success" behind, but this?

This feels better than sex on a copy machine.

With that, I leave you with one of my favorite quotes by Feynman, the man who is single-handedly responsible for redefining my grasp of what it means to be great. It's for mulling over. For comfort. And for reminding you that as long as you're living in the best way you know how, you don't owe anything to anyone.

"You have no responsibility to live up to what other people think you ought to accomplish. I have no responsibility to be like they expect me to be. It's their mistake, not my failing."

14

On Being Ferocious & Frothing At The Mouth, Akin To A Rabid Raccoon Named Jermaine

You are not exceptional. I'm not, either.

And before you go all ax-murderery and Google a picture of me so you can scratch my eyes out, this is actually a good thing. Because that means the only things separating you from everyone else? Are the choices you make.

It's not a matter of money, or inherent intelligence, or a genie that pops out of that dull lamp you found at the bottom of a sand dune shaped like a tiger's head. (Actually, in retrospect, one of those genies would be pretty handy. Let me know if you find one, okay? And then ask the genie if he has a brother I can date. Unlimited wishes, anyone?)

But back to the matter at hand.

You have two choices: give in to mediocrity, or fight (tooth and nail) for an exceptional life.

Because we all start out at ground zero. Within you, you have the ability to be an astronaut, or a leading advocate for women's rights, or a world traveler, or that guy from *Blue's Clues* who went to jail for drug possession.

And while I'll be the first to admit that it's easier, simpler, and more *la-dee-dah* pleasant to go with the flow, hit the snooze, and close the blinds? It's only through the hours and days and weeks and months and years of working relentlessly towards whatever it is you're working towards that lets you touch that fire. That finally sets your eyes alight. That allows you to crawl under the covers and fall asleep content, and proud, and ignited, at last. Because you've earned it, and your entire soul is tingling like it just had the best orgasm of its metaphorical life.

At the end of the day, WE'RE ALL JUST PEOPLE. And while we're people who are capable of more than anyone thinks possible, it's the active daily choices of deciding to live up to our potential, push past our limits and try just a little fucking harder that keeps us alive.

You have to choose to invest yourself into what matters most. Without that drive, you'll be unceremoniously shoved into a corner*, your fingers crammed in your ears and drool streaming down your chin.

*(Unless you're Baby, because no one puts Baby in a corner.)

And if you don't make that choice to show up, stand up, and speak up, you'll be left tuning out. Getting by. And settling for things you don't actually want, all the while knowing in your bones that you're missing out on the delicious feeling of living with a ferocity that just can't quite be defined.

You have it in you to be so much more than average. And it's time you fucking prove it.

15

On Midnight Trains To ~~Georgia~~ Pure, Undiluted Insanity

I'm really great at creating noise.

At finding anything to scoop out the silence and leave static humming in its place. Because humming doesn't hurt. Because noise doesn't negotiate. Because being in the total quiet means that my brain has free will. I can't control the weather. I can't control traffic. And—if it ain't the shit—I can't always control my thoughts.

Sometimes I worry that if I fall down when getting off the light rail and my knee splits open that all my secrets will come rushing out, scattered about the blood. That a passerby will stop (likely a man in khaki slacks), instinctively asking me if I'm okay as he wraps his hand around my upper arm and tries to tug me up before he sees the darkness spill on the pavement.

The hauntings. The untold stories. The bittersweet sludge that'll creep down the sidewalk and fill in the seams.

That I drove away my two best and longest friends over the last year during my depression, forcibly pushing them out of my life until they were too weary to accept the (many) invites back in, like dogs I'd beaten and left out in the rain. That sometimes I hold ice cubes in the palms of my hands until it hurts so badly I have to let go. That I cheerily chant, "early to bed, early to rise!" because staying up late makes me a *real* fucking weirdo.

I only ever write in the mornings. I type, as I write this in the dead of a Sunday night, hunched over the keyboard as a small fan perches on the edge of my desk, whirring as the train passes, and placating me with enough white noise that I don't need to crawl out of my skin. It keeps drying my eyes out, and I'm blinking more often than normal, the tiredness and constant air offsetting my body's balance. That's the thing about nights. They ruin balance.

In college, during a poetry workshop, I wrote something about that unsettling feeling of feeling too hard come midnight, and the teacher marked it through with her red pen. *Too cliché,* she scrawled in the comments.

At the time I was offended. Since then, I've found it endlessly comforting.

Because night has a way of making the shadows spark to life for everyone. Of bringing up every memory you've always tried to forget. Of leaving you raw, callously scrubbed raw from the day as the underpinnings of your personality start talking with each other, start shoving each other around, start asking the questions that you often drown out with the radio or the sounds of the train on its tracks out the window, clanging with the wind, or the murmur of voices from actors on TV as the flickering light makes it impossible to sleep, but so does the silence.

This was supposed to be funny. A sarcastic little diddy about the late-night ramblings of a pseudo-intellectual. Do people want to read that? Do people want to read this? Do people want to read what I have to say?

I acknowledge that I sound like a crazy person, but I can only accredit this to the fact that I am sort of a crazy person.

This feels like a drunken voicemail to an ex or a hell-bent Livejournal post circa 2003, when I'm hopped up on emotions I can't name that are pushing at the seams of my insides, trying to find a way out into the light.

Mostly, I think the nagging feeling of being completely unsettled comes with the worry that maybe I'll never have all the things I want. That maybe I don't actually know what the flying fuck I want. That I may never live up to my potential, or that I'm never doing enough, or that I'll never be enough. Is enough ever enough? Does doubting myself make you doubt me, too?

There's that worry. The spindling, winding worry of being loved by everyone, all the time, always. Once, I found out a group of people in a forum were talking about how my writing was "a waste of space" and that they "really didn't understand my worth" and I laughed to my boyfriend so hard I cried, and then cried so hard I dry heaved into our toilet, noting that it hadn't been cleaned in months, and then threw up among the existing filth. Because if they're putting that into the world, and if I ever dared say it aloud, would it become universally true?

Yesterday, I redecorated the apartment. Went out first thing in the morning and collected a haul around town, kicking the boyfriend out of the house for the day, and spending 13 hours straight painting walls and hanging up new pictures. Obsessively moving furniture around only to move it back to the same indentations in the carpet and finding comfort in things having their place. Forgetting to eat and drink and sit down and settle.

I needed new. I needed a fresh start. There's something in the water, something about spring that's racing through the air and making me want to scrub my hands clean of all the disastrous shit of this last year. We always talk about being vulnerable, how beautiful vulnerability is, but the fact of the matter is that it isn't always beautiful, because being vulnerable means being honest, and honesty can be really fucking ugly sometimes.

Sometimes I feel like a sham, someone going around and peddling snake oil at a fair, telling you that it'll be okay. Telling you that you'll be okay. Telling you that you are enough and you have enough and that eventually the thoughts will calmly quiet once you set them free, leaving just as they arrived—abruptly and without warning.

But if you get anything from this, know that I will always tell the truth.

Everything *will* be okay. And even if you have to step out onto your tiny balcony, look up at the stars you can't see, and wait for the train to get your thoughts back on track, you'll be able to settle back into yourself. Stop the secrets from spilling out to strangers.

Find strength in the simplicity that you're giving the world all you have, and that's all you have to give, isn't it?

When I was 14, I stumbled across a quote Henry David Thoreau wrote, that read, "The mass of men lead lives of quiet desperation." I memorized it immediately, if only so I could be the asshole who could effortlessly quote Thoreau at future imaginary parties. It used to get into my gut, that quote. Burrow deeply and rust there until I ached. *The mass of men lead lives of quiet desperation.*

But there's something stunning about it. A sense of serenity that comes when you realize and accept and embrace and laugh about the fact that we're all in this together. This insanely outlandish ride that has no definitive end, doing our best to do our best. The mass of men lead lives of quiet desperation, which means we are never, ever alone.

Now the train is coming.

And, in the spirit of honesty, I really need that noise.

16

On Eating Cold Cuts Soaked In Human Tears On The Carpeted Floor Of Your Grandparents' Parked RV

Confession: I readily skipped writing for a week. I had food poisoning from a Philadelphia Roll I'd left precariously perched on the edge of the counter for a few too many hours, and then hungrily scarfed down while watching a rerun of *Psych* in my underwear. (Sushi poisoning, you guys. It's messy.)

The next week, I was bombarded with a slew of annual check ups, having people jab at my hooha, scrape my teeth, and put an alarmingly cold stethoscope against my back.

The week after that? I lost someone important to me, and spent the week eating cold cuts while crying on an air mattress in an RV parked in my grandparent's driveway.

All "valid" excuses, right? I was sick. I was busy. I was hurting.

But somewhere along the line, that feeling of self-care and self-preservation transformed into crushing guilt. Molding, cloying awkwardness. Cringe-worthy heeby jeebies.

Without warning, writing went from something I looked forward to splashing into feet-first every week, frolicking about and dropping a few f-bombs...to that ex I have from college who's decided it's the very best idea to grow out waist-length dreadlocks and serenade me with *Offspring* songs on my voicemail every time he drinks too many lukewarm PBRs.

A month went by.

Sheepishly and shamefully, I watched deadline after deadline skate right on by, obnoxiously waving as they blurred past, decked out with hot pink tutus and tiaras like the smug little assholes they are. I sniffled into my Cocoa Dyno-Bites, letting the weight of the world crush my broad and sturdy shoulders in a way that gave me a constant tension headache. I made a rancid little home in the tightly wound ball of my excuses, refusing to open the blinds or drink anything that didn't include a liberal splash of gin.

More than anything? I thought about the perfect thing to say when I finally returned from my hiatus. I thought about saying I've been spending all my free time writing this book (blatant lie), exercising like a mad woman (kiiiiiiiind of true), and somehow saving the lives of thousands of people by solving the problem of clean drinking water (not true at all.)

But the fact of the matter is that I've been spending an inordinate amount of time reading the raunchiest romance novels I can get my pervy little hands on. Walking along rivers, and napping in the sun. Drinking sweet lattes and yelling at the screen in scary movies. I also seemed to spend approximately 3 hours vacuuming, if that counts.

This shit is embarrassing.

So why am I telling you this?

Because it's better to make mistakes than fake perfection.

It's better to say, "Hey. I effed up. My bad. What's next?"

It's better to look at your flaws, give them an uncomfortably long hug, and offer up heaping handfuls of acceptance.

You're going to goof up.

Let yourself down.

Get in your own way.

But what matters is how you recover. That incredible moment when you take a deep breath, and your new-found resolve starts thrumming through your bones, bouncing off the walls and resonating in your soul. When you realize you're ready to step up, despite the occasional slip.

When you accept that you—and your goals—are worth striving for day after day after finely flawed and magnificently messy day.

17

On Changing The World Without Going Back In Time And Killing Hitler

I'm interested in a world where Elvis played the tuba.

In this world where Elvis played the tuba, *The Rolling Stones* also played the tuba. Bob Dylan played the folksy tuba. The *Ramones* likely played dinged and dented tubas very loudly. And *The Beatles* played the tuba, as one would expect of *The Beatles,* in a yellow submarine.

But because one man, armed with a perfectly tailored white leather jumpsuit, decided to pick up an electric guitar instead of a tuba, he single-handedly shaped the entire future of music. (And for once, I'm not actually being overly dramatic.)

Because one man, swiveling his narrow hips, decided to run his fingers over the orderly and metallic strings of a guitar and not press in the tiny buttons on the side of a red accordion, he inspired millions of people—and still continues to inspire million of people—every single day with his smooth, crooning sounds.

And because one man, his inky black hair slicked away from his sweating forehead while the heat from the stage lights bore into his pores, concentrated on making the least popular choice?

He fucked with the future of the world.

We all know Elvis is an icon. Handsome, talented, and debonair—a deadly trifecta, if ever there was one. But besides his love for peanut butter and banana sandwiches, the most important thing about him?

He chose to literally rock an instrument that most critics of his time deemed at best to be a passing phase and at worst to be a grave annoyance. He saw the box he was expected to fit so neatly into, and hauled his taut tush in the other direction as fast as he possibly could.

He explored rock and roll, ultimately raking in the rolls of cash.

And while we can't all be Elvis (because let's face it—that white polyester jumpsuit caked with rhinestones would cause a serious swamp ass situation in the middle of June), we can choose to stray. To say no thank you to those outdated adages that have always governed how we go about getting things done.

When you conform to the course, you're making the path deeper, more weathered, more resistant to change.

But when you step out of stagnation, turn up the volume on your volition, and take one tiny nuanced step into the *never-befores*, you're changing the landscape of living. You're pushing new paths into fields of thigh-high wildflowers. You're picking up a guitar, sitting on the sidewalk with your feet in the rain-washed gutter, and reimagining what it means to make noise.

18

On Being An Unglamorous, Basic Bitch

I used to be really impressive.

In college, I was a mentor in the honor's program, and the founder of a university-wide film fest. On the weekends, I woke up in the dark, pinning my stylish straight-across bangs back with bobby pins before running my hands along the craggy rocks on the hike to the top of the Royal Arch, cracking open a Coors Light or two with friends as the light finally broke the horizon, sipping beers as the sun rose.

I directed plays, shattering donation records for a non-profit by the tens of thousands of dollars. Once, I literally had a guy stand underneath my dorm room window and serenade me with a song. I started a successful literary magazine.

But most importantly, I was happy and impulsive, carefree and adventurous.

I danced in sweltering clubs where my shoes stuck to the floor, letting my sweat mix with the sweat of other people. I drove across the country to sleep under the stars with 20,000 strangers on a whim, spending my days walking barefoot through an Oregon marsh and my nights around a bonfire, sipping tepid vegan broth. (Not one of my finest moments, mind you.)

I was always the one laughing the loudest. And I was always so confident in my steps and so sure of myself.

And in the future, I sometimes figure I'll be someone who wears perfectly tailored white slacks more days than not, expertly navigating through a majority of the major cities—New York, Paris, Milan—always knowing someone to ring up who will meet me for an overpriced drink in a hotel that's dripping with chandeliers and champagne.

I'll pen novels, magically becoming the sort of person who says *pens* instead of *writes*, probably favoring fountain pens over ballpoint, somehow managing not to let one single stray spot of black ink find its way to my pristine white pants.

I'll be most comfortable living from a suitcase and surrendering to serendipity, getting swept up in whatever northeastern breeze urges me to move mountains, move across rivers, move continents. I'll be effortlessly compassionate, completely content, and confident in my ability to take on the world, regardless of missteps or mistakes.

But right now, I'm Jess.

Instead of traveling, trekking across borders and making a life that's borderline impulsive, I'm spending more time in the sunlight and going to damn spin classes at the gym. I'm rigorously building a routine.

I'm most comfortable in $8 Target t-shirts and a pair of shorts I've owned for four years. Some days I fall asleep sure that I know where my feet will fall the next day, and some nights I never get to sleep, standing on my tiny concrete balcony and listening for the train.

Somewhere in the last 7 years, that certain, sugary-sweet, and eternally optimistic girl has become someone who has a tendency to scrawl out everything in a day planner (slick black ink, please). Who sometimes chooses to nap instead of careening down a dirt road to a tiny mountain town. Who occasionally worries that I've lost it—whatever *it* is, that used to make me so magnetic. But who knows that I'm finding my way back, finding my way forward, fighting my way forward into exactly who I want to to be.

Because sometimes, it takes unglamorous details, unglamorous choices to achieve those lofty goals.

And while, at this very second, I'd likely spill a Bloody Mary, (extra green olives), all over my white pants, there's something to be said for the freedom that's found in accepting exactly who you are, exactly in this moment, and finding rhythm in the process.

We're not has-beens, and we're not have-yet-to-bes.

We're just ourselves.

These bright, tangled wires of will and well-wishes, tumbling about until we find our footing in the best way we can. Walking along the waves on the North Carolina coast and knowing you're doing everything in your power to persevere. To perfect your passions. To become a powerhouse.

You might not be crusading with a caravan of hippies across the country anymore. Unlike the days of yore, you might not have suitors beckoning from beneath your windowpane (said in my best Shakespearean voice). You might not have timeshares in Tahiti yet. And you might not even be sure what your future success shakes out to look like.

But that doesn't mean you're not gearing up to cause one hell of a ruckus.

Because maybe you're learning the layout of the downtown Denver library by heart, or spending every evening walking through a rose garden, stopping to dangle your feet into a fountain where water pours out of a lion's mouth, old-school style. Maybe you drive three hours home on a Thursday morning, maneuvering down a winding highway with the windows down, finding a song to put on replay at least five times. Maybe you're drinking a gallon of spiked apple cider while sitting in the shade on one of those totally predictable red and white checkered tablecloths, weaving dandelions into crowns and tucking two neatly behind your left ear.

Do all of these things, if only so you can remember that

regardless of who you've been, and regardless of who you'll be, you can smile, let your chest collapse with an exhilarating exhale, and remember that life is GOOD. You are GOOD. You're moving forward. And you have the world sitting so seductively at your bare feet, between the jug of sun tea and a simple stack of well-worn books.

19

On Taking Tiny Steps Down An Even Tinier Brick Road

(probably with a microscopic flying monkey tangled somewhere in your hair)

Are you happy, or are you comfortable?

Does that sentence make you want to dry heave into the nearest empty fast food bag, too? (Oh, Wendy's $1 chili. WHY CAN'T I QUIT YOU?)

Those 7 words have caused me more 2 a.m. anxiety sessions, late afternoon outbursts (involving a fair number of snot bubbles and blubbering into an afghan), and general bodily discomfort than I'd care to recall.

Because it's something we all worry about. Momentum vs. stagnation. Progress vs. settling. Accomplishments vs. giving-in. And not to get too moody on you, but I have to whip out a lyric courtesy of Regina Spektor while introducing *Orange Is The New Black*. "Taking steps is easy. Standing still is hard."

I may have just thrust my fist aggressively into the air and shouted an ill-timed, *Preach, sister*! to an empty room. Let's allow a moment of silence to pity my neighbors.

But the question is valid. Where does happiness end and plain ol' comfort begin? Is there anything intrinsically wrong with comfort?

Can't we all be content and comfortable? (I'm pretty sure this is why yoga pants were invented, you guys.)

I'd like to think so.

The two aren't at war with each other, snapping down a dimly-lit alleyway and chanting the name of their gang Sharks vs. Jets style, and it's completely possible for the two to coexist, create a secret handshake, and even go out for a beer or 7, if I have anything to say about it.

However, the problem pops up after you wash your face at night. You splash the water onto your skin in the same way they do in cleanser commercials, essentially soaking your entire bathroom counter, and a large portion of your floor. Wiping the moisture from your cheeks and scrubbing at the remnant mascara smudges in the aggressive manner magazines warn you about, you look at yourself. Really take in the tiny tracks under your eyes. The small little curl on the right side of your face that you've had since you were born. The flecks of green scattered in your iris, and the nearly invisible freckles sprinkled over your shoulders.

And with a tungsten weight settling surely in your stomach, you lean in close to the mirror and whisper to your reflection staring back, watching your lips form the words and your crooked lower teeth reminding you of that year in middle school when you wore an unfolded paperclip in your mouth because all your friends had braces and you felt left out, muttering into the gentle and soap-scummed tile of your bathroom–

Am I doing the best I can?

Most nights, the answer will be yes. You'll be able to sneak a smile and crawl into your unmade bed, self-assured and ready for sleep. These are beautiful nights.

But sometimes, the answer is no, and it's all you can do not to run screaming through the streets, burning bridges before the sun breaks over the eastern skyline and tearing your hair out in tiny, inch-by-inch chunks, weaving them into some sort of totally *avant garde* living room rug and trying like hell to sell it on Etsy so you can afford to get extensions.

The truth—the intrinsic truth that echos around in our bellies like the chimes from determined and over-sized brass bells—is that we have *so* much potential. So much passion and possibility and power that it's enough to paralyze us where we stand, to let our feet spring roots securely into the soil and settle in to the weak streams of sunlight that illuminate the dust dancing in their wake.

All that said?

There's no shame in recognizing that you're not making all the moves you're capable of. That you're not taking every—or any—step in the direction you want to be going. That you're paralyzingly discouraged by a road block, a deep upheaval, or even the smallest of hiccups. Sometimes the motivation just doesn't materialize.

Yet it's when you embrace the flaws, scatter the shattered bits of who you've always thought you couldn't be, and welcome that fear that blows past you like a forceful autumn wind, that you're able to step into the place you've always wanted to be.

Don't cry over spilled milk. Don't punch yourself in the jaw over opportunities you passed up. (Probably don't punch yourself in the jaw *ever*, actually.) And don't let your past inaction keep you from acting on what you want.

Because that comfort and happiness is waiting for you.

All you have to do is trust that you have the talent, and take one tiny step in the right direction.

20

On Scarfing Down The Bullshit

(& then politely dabbing the corners of your mouth with a silk hanky)

My biggest fear has always been the idea of Bert Lahr living under my bed. Or more specifically, Bert Lahr when he played The Cowardly Lion in the 1939 classic *The Wizard of Oz*. (1939, you guys. BAFFLED.)

Something about that man in full lion makeup, leaping out of dimly-lit bushes and chuffing with his head of coiffed curls has literally made me cry from pure, unadulterated terror. Like, within the last five years.

Until my fourteenth birthday, I'd slap off the light switch by the door, sprinting like a damn Olympic runner across the low-shag purple carpet, and kicking off the ground so hard I'd soar Superman-style onto the bed–being sure to leave a buffer between my feet and the black space under my mattress so the lion man wouldn't wrap his gruff lion man hands around my ankles. (And for the record, I'm pretty sure Mumford & Sons' song *Little Lion Man* gave me post-traumatic stress disorder for just this reason.)

But now, if I were to perch on a bench in a rose garden, put my fist under my chin and stare longingly into the distance, looking both hauntingly beautiful and also vaguely constipated, I'd have to come to grips with my new more prevalent, (and logical) fear:

I'm terrified of believing my own lies.

I'm terrified of buying into my own Pinterest-perfect bullshit.

I'm terrified that my facade will be become fact.

And we're all running this risk all the time.

We say: "I don't care that he never wants to get married and chucked the wedding binder I've been compiling since I was 13 from cut-out pictures of *J-14 Magazin*e into a raging fire! I'm not the marrying type, anyways, and it's just an expensive party. We're fine. We're happy. I'm fine! I'm happy."

When we mean: "I'm settling for a relationship that's not what I want, and though it's going to hurt like hell, I have needs that aren't being met and standards that I won't compromise on. I'm going to be fine. I'm going to be happy. But I need to make a change."

We say: "My tonsillectomy was great! It was so wonderful to

unwind and catch up on movies and get some well-deserved reading done. I really appreciate the opportunity to just relax, you know? I'm grateful."

When we mean: "I was alone in my dirty apartment for 13 days, barfing so hard it was spewing out my nose and stinging the gaping, lasered holes in my throat, and I was in such intense pain I couldn't follow the plot of anything, let alone even attempt to read a book. Also? The constant flow of Percocet through my system gave me the most graphic and unsettling sex dreams about the man so famously known as Mr. Rogers. (The things he can do with his bowtie.)"

We say: "I'm lucky to have my job! It's not perfect, but then again, nothing is. I have benefits and health insurance, and I'm just so thankful to have the opportunity. I have a real future at the company, and I love that strangers walk by my desk, rap their knuckles on the cheap particle board, and say, 'Smile!' at least 37 times a day. It's a great reminder to be optimistic!"

When we mean: "I don't love my job. I know what job I'm going to love more, and I'm going to go after it. I smile plenty, *thank you,* and while I might have a future at the company, I have a brighter future on my own. Things could be worse, but things could be better, and I'm ready to explore my pure potential."

Bad guys under our beds are legitimately terrifying, but the scariest thing?

It's when our pleasant niceties become non-fiction. When we've successfully brainwashed ourselves. And when we've nonchalantly dumped a huge brimming bucket of *it's-fine-I'm-fine-everything's-fine* on that fire that smolders just beneath the surface. That urges us to strive for success, push our potential, and fistfight our way to the best fucking futures possible.

Keeping up appearances is fine and dandy(lions). But don't let your image get in the way of what you can imagine.

21

On Being A Damn, Dirty Thief

On the last day of 5th grade, I had my first kiss.

Or to be totally honest, I stole it. My best friend in the whole world, Chris, was walking down the narrow schoolbus aisle two stops before mine, his backpack hitting the faded brown leather seats in a rhythmic pattern. Just as he passed my seat, I basically yelped. "Chris! I have a secret to tell you!" I even did the little wiggling thing with my finger to make him lean in closer.

And as I went in for what he presumed was a light whisper in his ear, I sneak-attacked that son of a gun, whipping my head around to the front of his face and planting a very firm, fast, and closed-lipped kiss square on his mouth.

He looked at me for a second, hiked his navy canvas Jansport higher up on his back, and nodded. "Okay," he said. "See you."

We spent most of that summer before middle school holding hands at Skate City and slow roller skating (which is the preteen version of slow dancing, obviously), to TLC's *No Scrubs.* My hands were mostly sweaty and holding his in a death grip. The place between his pointer finger and thumb was always chapped. Sometimes we drank out of the same straw when we pooled the change in our pockets and bought a Sprite from the concession stand while awkwardly staring at the black velvet carpet that was laced with neon stars.

Basically, I was buzzing with adrenaline for months, smiling like someone whose smiler dial was broken, and trying my damndest not to paint a mural on the living room wall that just said, "I KISSED A BOY! I SORT OF HAVE A BOYFRIEND!" And then I would have also painted a sun wearing sunglasses, because I was really into suns wearing sunglasses and drawing those elaborate diamond Ss where you made 6 vertical lines and connected them in a way that made an ordinary letter look like sweet, gangster-ass graffiti.

And that adrenaline, that magnetic pull that starts in my toes—with the chipping magenta polish and nonexistent pinky toenails—making me want to literally, physically stretch up towards the sky and grasp onto a molten, burning star, regardless of the sting in my palm or the unlikelihood of success—has followed me my entire life. It's like being haunted by the ghost Charlie Chaplin, except less silent-film-star and way more motivational.

It's that carnal, deep-rooted feeling that there's something incredible, just beyond my reach.

That there's something more, hanging out at the very edge of the periphery of my comfort zone.

That if I run at full speed towards the edge of the world and just LEAP, I won't fall off, drift aimlessly into space, and wind up getting sucked into a black hole (and likely spaghettified), but rather have one of those rare, completely undiluted moments of full-body bliss.

Looking back on successes makes me crave more good.

Sometimes, when I'm on the freeway, windows down on my 2004 white Honda Accord (that almost always needs a good washing), and it's one of those lucky days when my stereo works without me having to punch the top of my dash with the force of Thor's hammer, *No Scrubs* will come on. A throwback to the '90s? You bet your sweet bippy.

But also a reminder of how those little glimpses of the (pleasant) past remind of us who we are. Of where we've been, and where we have the potential to go. (Also, Skate City is totally still open. I technically have the potential to go there.)

It's all about those small snippets of time, 14 years later, when your heart is full and the sun is warming your left arm as it hangs out the car window and the wind tangles your hair into eleventy billion knots and how you know, just know that the smell of Bubblegum Smackers chap stick will always make Chris remember how you squinched up your eyes and laid one on him on the last day 5th grade.

Twelve year-old Jess learned a valuable lesson.

Sometimes, you can't wait for the ship to come to shore—you have to swim out and meet it.

Sometimes, you can't wait for the perfect career to fall into your lap—you have to build a website to get the CEO's attention.

And sometimes, you can't wait for a boy to give you your first kiss.

Sometimes? You have to steal it.

22

On Decisions Being Malevolent, Manipulative Little Shits

(not unlike Rebecca in 3B who guilts you into attending all of her book club meetings that only read obsolete tech manuals from 1993)

An atheist walks into a bar and downloads five different tarot cards apps to her phone.

This isn't the start to a joke—it's what I did last night. Because when I'm faced with any sort of decision, the anxiety of choice settles into my stomach like handfuls of moldy aquarium rocks, weighing on my mind (and probably making me weigh more on the scale, too. *Looks around innocently.*)

To move when my lease is up, or not to move? To wake up early and go for a jog around the lake, or to sleep in? To eat mint Oreos for dinner, or to have the last few bites of cranberry sauce? TO BATHE OR NOT TO BATHE?

Ridiculous, right?

But before I know what's happening, my shoulders are velcroed to my ears and there's a persistent throbbing right between my shoulders blades that aches with each and every rapid-fire heartbeat. With each choice comes entirely separate narratives of possibilities and outcomes, spidering out like cracked glass and creating complicated webs of wondering. It's exhausting, all that wondering and worrying all the time.

That's what it comes down to, after all. Worry. Fear. *Gosh*, the fear.

What if I make the wrong choice? IS there a wrong choice? And if there isn't a wrong choice, which choice is better? Is any choice better? But what does my GUT say? And my family? And the damn tarot card app?!

It's like being in a fun house, the strategically placed mirrors distorting reality and making you queasy with discomfort. It's unfamiliar territory, and the future can seem like the most terrifying place on the entire planet. (Unless you're locked in that kitchen from *Jurassic Park* with velociraptors. That's likely more terrifying.) It's so easy to get sucked into the quicksand of feeling like you have no idea what the fuck you're doing, or are going to do, or should do.

It makes us feel vulnerable, and fragile, and unsure of ourselves.

Hell, it's enough to drive a person to drink. (Small batch whiskey. Neat.) And it's certainly enough to make us turn to tarot and psychics and coin flips and 2 a.m. hysterical calls to our friends and so, so many separate pro/con lists and did I mention whiskey?

And yet, at the end of the day, all that stuff is just noise. Distractions from what we actually want. Scapegoats for the feelings in our guts.

We've become so afraid of knowing what we want and going after it when those visceral and certain wants are what keep us alive.

Because when we choose for ourselves, the repercussions of those choices fall solely on us, the good and bad piling up in our palms and pooling at our feet.

But it's not just about choosing *for* ourselves. It's about choosing ourselves, completely.

About knowing we're strong enough to shoulder the backlash, humble enough to reap the rewards, and resilient enough to try again.

Decisions aren't pressure to choose between right and wrong. They're just pure, naked, raw seconds in our timelines that grant us the opportunity to inch a little closer to what we want. To choose our own adventure. To plod on down whichever path makes our pulses pull off a perfect pirouette. (Or at least complete a successful cycle of *The Macarena.*)

And as for me? I just want a bubble bath, and for you to know that no matter what, you'll come out on top*.

**Insert sex joke.*

23

On Suicide, Depression & Shitting Your Pants

In the third grade, I shit my pants.

After a hot lunch of wet mashed potatoes heaped onto a scratched and red plastic tray, it was time for The Presidential Fitness Challenge. (Cue the fanfare.)

As it was an opportunity to earn a blue ribbon that would color coordinate nicely with the others on the bulletin board hanging above my daybed, I approached the challenge much in the way I approach any and every friendly game of Monopoly: with unwarranted ferocity and a wad of fake paper money shoved down the front of my pants.

So, as my partner unsuspectingly held my feet while I huffed, puffed, and did as many sit ups in 120 seconds as humanly possible, a teeny, tiny fart bubble escaped. I felt my cheeks flush, but chose to ignore it.

Then the cramps started. Deep, aching contractions in my guts. And before I knew what was happening, my body had become an ass volcano, poop pouring into my light grey shorts as my partner stared down in horror. Not knowing what else to do, I kept up the crunches, each sit up uncannily resembling squeezing the end of a toothpaste tube. (Whenever you think it's empty, just roll up the end, and magically, more appears.) I was a study in humiliation, a human toothpaste tube incapable of not spraying diarrhea everywhere.

Walking home from the bus stop that day, wearing oversized basketball shorts from the lost and found and my shitty shorts (pun intended) secured tightly in a plastic grocery bag swinging at my side, I wanted to disappear. I wanted to sink into non-existence. I wanted to erase that moment in time when my gym teacher came over to look at the commotion, only to shove his fist in his mouth and yell, "OH, SWEET JESUS!"

I was pretty sure I'd never want to just die as much as I did that day.

I was wrong.

Enter, stage left: Depression.

That sneaky little asshole who burrows into your brain and whispers vicious nothings in your ear until you're literally aching with apathy.

Depression lies—just like that time I convinced my little brother he could get high from huffing farts.

But consider this permission to seek refuge. To find a quiet place of safety where you can shit your pants to your heart's content. (And I pinky promise there will be no shouted expletives that echo across the rubbery orange gym floor.)

Find a place to cry, hard and loudly. To make snot bubbles the size of small children and high-pitched screeches that only dogs can hear.

To explore, endure, help, and heal.

I'm writing you from a comforter cocoon on my couch with the blinds closed on a damn dreary Denver day after mainlining nearly an entire box of Kraft spiral macaroni and cheese straight out of the sauce pan. (Real talk: the spiral kind just tastes so much better, you guys.)

The bottom line? I've always been depressed. Since I was 15, I've been to therapists, psychologists, and support groups. I've been on meds, off meds, drank herbal tea, and meditated. (Spoiler: When my brain tries to go quiet it just starts playing every Ke$ha song I've ever heard on repeat, complete with bass beats and synthesizers.)

Most of the time it's manageable.

Most of the time, I feel "normal," have a little skippity-doo-dah in my step and enough good will to be able to make jokes with the check out clerk at the grocery store. Most of the time, I get a "normal" amount of sleep, have a "normal" day of productivity, and cry a "normal" amount. Most of the time I can function.

But sometimes all the crying stops and I find myself fresh out of feelings—any feelings—about anything, and can't seem to scrape up the energy to actually shower, so instead I drag my sorry ass into the bathtub and turn on the tap, squeezing a borderline obscene amount of soap into the rushing water in the hopes that ALL THE BUBBLES will somehow buoy my spirits. I don't sleep. I bury myself balls-deep into work.

And I spend a fair amount of time lying on the floor, staring at the ceiling, and wondering how much time it would take to grow my armpit hair long enough to be able to braid it because *nothing* in the world matters, let alone things like shaving my body. (This, of course, is all happening amidst crushing feelings of anxiety and existential musings that mostly make me want to curl up in a ball like a damn adorable (adamnable?) Pokémon character and never return to the real world.)

The bottom line?

I get it. Mental illness.

(*Illness* being the key word here.) I've been on both sides, and just about everywhere in between. (Except for Nantucket. Never been to Nantucket.)

And if you've never felt like you're not good enough—

Never felt like you're not worth enough—

Never felt like life doesn't have enough meaning (or any meaning, on the worst days)—

Never felt so hard it hurts, while simultaneously throbbing with aching emptiness—

Then you can meander your magnificent ass to a different chapter and check back in later. (I'll be here with bells on. Literal bells. That can play *Twinkle, Twinkle, Little Star.*)

But if you need a little love, a snack-sized snuggle, and a perfectly-timed pick me up, I've totally got you. The Hole sucks (that annoying place that always smells cloyingly of moldy leaves and only plays *Full House* reruns nonstop on a static-y TV).

And I can't blow unlimited amounts of sunshine up your ass with a bendy straw, but I can tell you with certainty that some day, sometime, something will matter to you in a way that helps you make it through another damn day and maybe even smile a little.

Whatever you're going through is not the end, and there will always be someone (HI!) on the other side, ready to lead you into the sunlight and set off a damn confetti cannon to commemorate the exceptional creature THAT IS YOU.

You're stronger than the sadness. Depression is not a death sentence. And The Hole can't hold you.

You're going to make it through this.

And that, ladies and gentlemen? Is a motherfucking promise.

24

On What Seeing Thousands Of Boobs Taught Me About Myself

I've seen more boobs than the average person.

The summer after I turned 21, I drove halfway across the country with an ex from high school, each of us taking turns at the wheel of the car we weren't *quite* sure would make it to Washington state and drinking yogurt out of a bottle. We listened to the fastest tempo music at the loudest volumes so we wouldn't doze off and hit one of the (eleventy billion) freight trucks that were racing along the same highways as us.

We were headed to The Rainbow Gathering, a huge gathering of...erm...*free spirits* who traipse around in mother nature in different parts of the US each year, worship the earth, do a lot of drugs together, and poop in big groups. But more on this later. After three days of sleeping in a locked car at rest stops with my feet jammed up to my chest and liberally spraying dry shampoo eeeeeeeverywhere, we finally made it to The Gathering spot—an elusive little bastard tucked up in the mountains of Spokane. (After getting lost for hours on winding dirt mountain roads, we finally fell in behind a pickup truck packed with people wearing rainbow bandannas, so we stuck with them.)

Pulling into the huge makeshift parking lot, it was immediately clear to me that I'd made a huge mistake. There was still snow on the ground, despite it being mid-summer. The beat up cars had windows white with weed smoke literally as far as the eye could see, and at 9 o'clock in the morning, there were already men pushing 80, camped out on faded red canvas chairs at the trailhead, drinking warm PBRs and scratching the matted fur behind their dogs' ears.

I hauled my huge pack out of the back of the car and strapped myself in, fighting that screaming voice in my gut to TURN AROUND AND GO THE HELL HOME, YOUNG LADY.

But I persisted. I told myself that I'd only grow by being outside of my comfort zone. That my fear was going to be *transformative*. That I had to push myself past my boundaries. And that the warning voice was actually an encouragement to move forward.

So I hiked the 7 miles into camp, stopping along the way in makeshift tents made of huge colorful tarps strewn between trees for a cup of tea that I drank out of an empty soup can. I wobbled my way across logs that were laid across rivers to connect these chunks of wet, muddy marshes that made up the entire area. And I passed group after group of people totally fucked out of their minds.

Within the first five minutes of making it into the main camping area, my travel buddy (who had basically made me a blood pact he wouldn't leave me alone for a single second during the trip) disappeared into a drug haze, and I didn't see him for the next four days.

Not really knowing what else to do, I found the most level spot of marsh I could, laid down the "waterproof" tarp, and set up a tent for the first time in my life. And listening to the tent 10 feet to my left have continuous and absurdly loud sex for hours and hours on end, I cried and cried and cried, only taking a break long enough to hike into the trees to find the latrine that I'd heard rumors of.

Few things are quite as humbling as sitting on a log with your butt hanging over the edge, pooping into a dug out hole with 20 other people, all of them making very intense eye contact and talking casually about your black and white flannel.

(My black and white flannel was a topic of many conversations since I was in the 5% of women at The Gathering actually wearing a shirt. Like I said, I've seen a *looooooot* of boobs. Lopsided boobs. Boobs that looked cross-eyed. Perky ones and ones that hung mid-stomach. Ones decorated elaborately with henna, and ones with bite marks on the side. Boobs, you guys.)

The next week was a blur. My tent flooded every night, so I spent 8 pm to 6 am shivering and soaking wet, and then the days laying out my sleeping bag and clothes into the damp sunny patch of grass in front of my spot, sleeping mostly naked in the humid tent as the hot mid-day sun evaporated all the rain from the night before. And still, my tent neighbors continued to have enthusiastic sex.

When I was hungry, I'd wander around directionless until I found one of the food stations, the closest one being a place that served vegan broth that was the same temperature as my body, and it was customary to sit around a burning fire as the sun was burning down, sipping out of dirty bowls and scooping chunks of tomato and raw onion into your mouth.

When I was bored, I'd go to Trade Circle, a huge swap meet in the center of the campsite where people could trade with each other for just about anything and everything, as long as no money passed between hands. (Money's not allowed in The Rainbow Gathering.) I saw more than one person give away *all* of their clothes for a melted snack-sized Snickers bar.

I watched people dance around drum circles. Listened to people play guitars at varying levels. Girls hula hooping, their boobs also somehow hula hooping. Journaled a lot. Talked to people named Moon Flower and Strawberry Cloud. Walked barefoot through the marshes, the mud creating protective layers on the bottom of my feet. Picked up ants the size of my pinky and just held them there between my pointer finger and thumb, watching their legs squirm before setting them back down in the dirt and letting them scurry off.

And in between all of this, I cried some more. Because I *wanted* to love it. I wanted to be a topless girl with a tambourine, dancing around the firelight with a joint hanging easily from my lips, my filthy, dirty hair waving about in the cool night air and telling strangers that my name was Starlight Sprinkles with a completely straight face. I *wanted* to be free and reckless. I *wanted* to be one of the romantics. Fuck, I wanted to want it.

But I didn't. I was miserable. It wasn't just about being dirty or cold or hungry. The drum circles felt stupid. The stories all sounded the same. And all these people so hellbent on connecting were so desperately clinging to whatever drug was nearest to blur the boundaries between dreams and reality.

That's the best way to put it, really. It was running onto the set of a world I'd pictured myself being a part of for so long, and then realizing it was actually a horror film—*not* a profound Jack Kerouac novel. I passed on drugs, sat in big groups of people having the exact same "deep" conversation on repeat as we all "connected" in a "profound way," crawling back into my tent each night feeling hollow and sick.

I had gone to find and connect with (what I thought was) my truuuuuuue self, while it seemed like everyone else was trying to escape the real world.

I'd been there a week, and there were still 3 days left of The Gathering. I woke up in the morning before the sun, and quietly packed up the wet tent, stuffing everything into my pack and strapping in. It was The Morning of Silence, where everyone gathered in The Gratitude Circle (where we all prayed to the Earth and chanted together every night at supper to get chunks of bread), but this morning was different. The Morning of Silence meant everyone in child's pose, their foreheads pressed to the wet marsh as they hummed. Even the birds knew to pipe the fuck down.

And I snuck out. I snuck out like a damn thief, my feet making tiny squelching noises in the mud with my tennis shoes draped around the back of my neck, the laces knotted together so I could reach them easily when I made it into the woods for the hike out. Everyone was at The Gratitude Circle, and I made it back to my car without encountering a single human being.

Driving home, I thought about how surreal it all was. (It still IS surreal. I reread the journal entries I wrote and can't believe it's something I did, or thought I'd want to do.) And pulling up in front of my house, I sprinted towards the shower, the steam reeking like the smell of wet dog, and then promptly went out for sloppy ribs with my boyfriend. Full disclosure: I ate *a lot* of ribs.

I'm telling you all of this because we don't always know who we are.

We have this romantic, picturesque idea of who we think we are. Of who we'd like to be. Of who we'd like to think we are.

But in 7 days, I shattered an illusion I'd been carrying with me for years. And I can say with certainty, five years later, that I'm not a free spirit. I'm not someone who enjoys long stints of camping and interactions relying solely on the personalities of strangers. I'm not someone who wants to hula hoop, drink out of soup cans, or live off of thin, watery broth. I am not the Manic Pixie Dream Girl. I'm a real person.

I have important conversations with people who are important to me, and ridiculous conversations with them too, because those conversations are just as essential. I like the feeling of ripping meat off bones with my teeth. I like privacy when I shit. I like my warm, dry bed with the decorative pillows and an evening cocktail off my new bar cart. I like being outside when I want to be outside. I like cell service. I like working in well-lit coffee shops and blogging. And I like having a home.

I am not a nomad.

This doesn't make me shallow. It doesn't make me materialistic. It doesn't make me less. It doesn't make me incapable of experiencing the world in the ways that matter most to me. It just makes me who I am.

You don't have to be who you think you want to be. You don't have to be who you think you are. You just have to be *you*.

Because I promise when you're careening down a mountain and smelling like a goat, every cell in your body will know that *you don't fit where you don't fit*. You don't like *what you don't like*. You are not who you are not.

And as soon as you let go of that nagging pressure to hold onto your ideals? You finally become free to LIVE, JUST AS YOU ARE. (And also use a bathroom with a door. Because if there's one thing I've learned, it's not to underestimate the power of pooping in private.)

25

On Feet That Would Make Fred Flintstone Dry Heave Into The Nearest Skull Of A Dead Brachiosaur

My feet belong to a very broad, very masculine, hair-encrusted caveman.

Wide and absurdly flat, I'm relatively sure they'd make loud and vaguely accosting slapping sounds if I ran barefoot on concrete. The soles that should be so delicate, soft, and ready to make their appearance in a stunning pair of six-inch stilettos are padded with a thick layer of yellowed callouses—a barrier against heaping piles of summers walking on white hot sands, autumns spent striding barefoot over stacks of tangled and fallen leaves, winters wet and drying out by the fire, and springs picking my way over cold riverbeds.

And as for my heels? My heels are thick and dry, dirt packed into the cracks that spindle out like lines on a shattered sheet of glass.

But, though ugly and worn, aching and caked, my feet are durable, resilient, and strong.

Because by being exposed to the same elements over and over, year after year, they've learned their weak points and adapted. They've memorized the fleeting feeling of seashells tumbled to sand, jagged edges poking into the thin skin covering the bottom of my gentle, sloping arches. They've noted the not-so-pleasant sting of hot hardwood stamping itself into the soles of my feet as I ran repeatedly across my grandparents' deck, chasing after the dog who was chasing after my niece who had four hot dogs clutched in her fist and taken off squealing.

My feet defend themselves against danger, have put up a thick guard between themselves and the ground.

Yet there's something to be said for soaking the weathered patches in huge, bubbly suds. For sloughing away the roughness. For stripping down to the bare strips of soft skin. (Just as there's something to be said for the slight pain of the pebbles on the bottom of a mountain stream and the way fine grit grinds into your toes.)

But the barriers build. The defenses get more difficult to disable. And shutting down, shutting others out, and shutting ourselves in feels natural, easy, and ever at the ready.

We all want to be tough.

We want to walk across the scathing surface of the sun without the semblance of a seer, our layers of skin perfectly pristine in their hardened strength. We strive to remain unmarked by monumental adventures, callous to relationship catastrophes, and immune to setbacks, let downs, and failures.

And while it's easier to ignore the sharp stabs from the pointed corners of smashed shells, it's important to strip down, breathe deep, and dive in.

Because it's not about avoiding those tears between our toes, the abrasions on our ankles and the deep, resounding ache in the arches our our feet. It's about embracing them. Hauling ass into the Atlantic Ocean every year like ticking & tocking clockwork, not in spite of that scar that trims our left leg from a jellyfish sting from the summer we turned twenty-three, but because of.

As my six year-old little sister has precociously proclaimed while battling an intense splinter situation, "I don't like anything that causes me pain," but it's that pain that reminds us where we've been.

It reminds us what we've been through.

And it reminds us where we're capable of going.

26

On Being A Drunk Douchebag

Brace yourself, because it's about to get touchy (and also) feely up in this bitch.

New Year's Eve, I got in a raging fight with the boyfriend, the sort where we were huddled in a corner of a bustling party, whisper yelling (totally a thing) at each other and physically shaking from anger. I'd had enough to drink that I shouldn't have been discussing anything other than what burrito I wanted from Taco Bell on the way home, but alas, these things happen to the best of us (or at least the stupidest of us), especially on national holidays.

I won't go into the gory details, but I will say that it was dramatic, and it was rushed, and when he left me alone in my bed after the clock unceremoniously struck midnight (my updo looking like I'd styled it with that fork from *The Little Mermaid* and eye makeup streaked across my cheeks), he turned in the doorway, back-lit and handsome, and said, "So. Are you going to apologize?"

And I stubbornly squared my shoulders, looked him in the eye and snapped, "Nope. I meant every word. And that's all I've got."

Note: Tired, emotionally-drained and vaguely drunk Jessica has the capacity to be a raging asshole, but we all knew that, right?

Unable to sleep, I stumbled towards the Advil and flopped on my couch, my living room warmly lit. I'd been on the east coast for the last six weeks, and knowing that I'd miss Christmas at home, the boyf had come over the night before, setting up a tree and decorating it with the ornaments he's been collecting since he was a kid. He draped lights across the windows and put stuffed snowmen on the table, and I can say with certainty that is one of the nicest and most thoughtful things anyone has ever done for me.

We were supposed to have Christmas together after the party, but instead I decided to corner him in a house we'd never been to, jabbing my finger in his face and saying words that should probably never be said to your enemy, let alone to someone you actually care about.

Wordlessly, I sat in front of the tree, removing each small ornament and tucking them safely into a plastic grocery bag. Sighing, I unplugged the lights and unwound them from the windows. And bitterly, I shoved the tree into the coat closet. Out of sight, out of mind. Out of sight, off my conscience.

IF ONLY LIFE WAS THAT EASY.

The moral of this story?

We all fuck up.

Sometimes, it's in big ways like screaming at our boss to shove their new stapler up their overly-paid ass, and sometimes it's in smaller ways like not holding the door for someone behind us. But we all mess up, sort of all of the time. Life is an ongoing cycle of trip-ups and mistakes, of let-downs and harsh words.

But what matters is how we fix it. The way we choose to rebuild bridges we've set fire to, admit our faults, and ask for forgiveness.

The boyf and I sorted through it like most things I try to valiantly destroy. I apologized profusely and threatened to write a sonnet where I compared him to a summer's day. I explained what I was feeling and why I lashed out. And I vowed to do better. But most importantly?

I pulled out the tree and the lights, slowly rehung each ornament, and thanked every god I've ever thought about believing in that people are flawed creatures—always capable of bitterness and meanness and scorn, but also brimming with hope, and forgiveness, and light.

The tree looks great. The New Year is just starting. And while we're all going to royally screw it up? We'll also find ways to repair the holes. To learn from our mistakes. To be better people each and every day. Every screw up is an opportunity to suck less. It's a lesson in growth, and a chance for change.

So here's to us and our inevitable mistakes. Let's find a little more humanity, a little more humility, and a little more humor along the way.

27

On Answers To Unanswerable Questions

1. Which came first: the chicken, or the egg?

The chicken and the egg came simultaneously. The chicken laid the magically fertilized egg, kept it warm, and when the little egg hatched, the mom chicken and baby chicken became really close friends who exchanged scathingly witty dialogue in the small Connecticut town of Stars Hollow before Rory left and went to college. (Oh, wait. That's the plot to *Gilmore Girls*. My bad.)

2. Why do we say tuna fish, but not crow bird or bear mammal?

Because tuna fish are pretentious assholes who like to feel distinguished, and bear mammal sounds ridiculous.

3. If a tree falls in a forest, and there's no one around to hear it, does it still make a sound?

Yes. Obviously. Just because no one's around doesn't mean that the forest warps into some weird parallel universe where huge chunks of wood crashing into the ground don't make any noise. Also, Katniss is probably in that forest, so no tree will ever go unheard ever again.

4. How do you fit a square peg into a round hole?

Make sure the square peg is really tiny, and the round hole is really big. BLAMO.

5. If Peter Piper picked a peck of pickled peppers, where is the peck of pickled peppers Peter Piper picked?

Probably at his house. Peter Piper wasn't just going around, buying pecks of pickled peppers and throwing them on the ground or giving them as gifts. He wasn't a pickled pepper baron, buying the peppers and handing 'em out like candy. He probably just needed to add some flavor to his old-timey stew.

6. If your friends jumped off a cliff, would you?

Probably, but that's because I'm easily influenced and love a good adrenaline high.

7. Is the sky actually the limit?

Definitely not. There's all sorts of planets and space shit beyond the sky.

8. Do blondes really have more fun?

I mean, they seem to always be laughing in commercials, so... yes. The final answer is yes.

9. How much wood could a woodchuck chuck if a woodchuck could chuck wood?

So, woodchucks don't actually "chuck" or throw wood, but they do chew on it, so let's pretend that "chuck" and "chew" mean the same thing in this instance, okay? And according to numerous studies, woodchucks chuck about 361.9237001 cubic centimeters of wood per day, per woodchuck.

10. Can you actually paint with all the colors of the wind, à la Pocahantas?

Yes! Assuming you're on LSD.

11. If oranges are called oranges, why aren't bananas called yellows?

Actually, the word orange comes from the the Tamil words *aru* meaning six, and *anju,* meaning five. Since oranges usually have 11 little pieces inside, when you cut them in half, there are six pieces in one half and five in the other. The color was probably named after the fruit, so yellow should really be called banana.

Also, the English language is WACK.

12. Do April showers bring May flowers?

Yes, and also allergies, because *science*.

13. Who let the dogs out?

I did. Just this morning, actually, because they were whining at the door and I didn't want them to let loose a poop fountain on my new Ikea duvet...again.

14. Why did the chicken cross the road?

To make people stop asking this stupid fucking question.

15. Is gullible really written on the ceiling?

I promise you, it isn't. Don't check and see if it's there, because then everyone will laugh at your expense and you'll have to comfort yourself by eating a meatball Hot Pocket in the bath.

16. How much is that doggy in the window?

I mean, at least $350 since pet stores are so expensive. Try going through a rescue, instead!

17. If there are A batteries, and C batteries, why aren't there B batteries?

There actually used to be B batteries, but they're just not usually sold anymore since they tend to be the same size and volts as most A batteries. (CASE CLOSED.)

18. How many licks does it take to get to the center of a Tootsie Pop?

On average, over 800 licks. Just bite that son of a bitch, and save yourself the trouble, (and bloody tongue wounds).

19. When the someone knock-knocks, who's actually there?

Dwayne. Dwayne who?, you might ask. DWAYNE THE BATHTUB! I'M DWOWNING!

Kidding—I can't type and drown at the same time, you guys.

20. How many seashells did Sally sell by the sea shore?

Probably zero, because the business model is terrible. Why on earth would you try and sell something on the beach that people can literally pick up off the ground for free? GET YOUR SHIT TOGETHER, SALLY.

28

On Meditating Without Feeling Like A Total Asshole

Cleaning my kitchen changed my life.

There I was, scouring the counters with a Mister Clean Magic Eraser and listening to a Top Hits radio station, letting the gentle sweat seep into my hairline as I worked in tight, methodical circles. I erased the strawberry juice from my breakfast. I erased the splatters of sauce from week-old sloppy joes. I erased the weird ring of rust that always creeps up around the rim of my sink.

And as a song I hated came on, trailing quietly in from the living room and being as unassuming as possible, I snapped.

Slamming my fist on the counter top, I shouted out loud to no one, "That's it. I'm done fucking around." (This moment is actually what catalyzed a new tagline for my blog, if we're being totally honest with each other.)

And nothing's been the same since.

I've changed so much in the last two months that it freaks me the eff out. Like, genuinely scares me if I think too hard about it after the sun has set and my tea has cooled. (Peppermint tea. Let's get precise.)

Somehow, my life has become less about clinging to ideas of who I should be, and more about letting go of the loose ends. It's less about clawing my way into positions of power, and more about working smarter, letting my accomplishments speak soundly and sweetly for themselves. It's less about aggression and more about acceptance, talking with more purpose, and less volume.

Now, I'm not saying I'll serenely sprawl out in the middle of a freshly-paved road and exhale peacefully, willing "whatever will be to be." Because that horseshit is a direct train to Mediocre Town, population: you. Or at the very least, getting whacked by a vintage VW Bug going fifteen over the speed limit.

But it's so easy to start festering, letting the negativity seep into each and every crack and grow like the worst case of fungus you've ever seen. (Athlete's foot, maybe? Athlete's foot is pretty terrible.)

You might find yourself fighting. Hell, you might be starting fights, all in the name of accomplishing something.

As a result? You spend so much energy spinning your wheels, spitting at your reflection, and turning into a black hole of a human being.

And then maybe something important breaks inside you and the anger bubbles up, spilling out over the linoleum tile and causing deep, uncomfortable fissures in your oh-so-consciously-crafted facade.

Suddenly, all you want is to sit in the quiet. To stretch out your taut and tightly wound shoulder muscles and let the breathing make your chest bloom. You want a break from yourself—from the endless loop of *I need to*s and *I should*s and *What if I just can't*s. From the fear, and the fighting, and being fraught in a fever-pitch frenzy of frustration that comes with that haunting hollering in your brain that maybe you're not doing enough. Never enough. Never well enough.

The brain can be a little bitch, sometimes.

So, and this is an order, let yourself sit.

Turn off the radio and sit on your unvacuumed carpet. Feel the dull and repetitive ache in your lower back flood into the floor. Sit and let the silence sink in. Sit and try to surrender to the serenity, because struggling against yourself hasn't been doing you a damn bit of good.

A welcomed spell of daily silence where you run your habits and relationships and checklist by your gut, letting yourself test out each thought and clue you in as to what will feel best—as to what is best.

For me, as I've recently discovered, this means never letting the sunrise beat me out of bed. It means letting go of relationships that have run their course, opening up great expanses of space for new ones to grow like damn dandelions, reaching for the summer sun. It means hour-long workouts. Making less late-night Taco Bell runs and more book clubs. Less booze. More binge watching gritty detective crime dramas. (I'm lookin' at you, *True Detective.*) Filling up my well that had seemed so dry for so long with words and rhythms and writing.

Because at its base, change means sitting with that silence, consciously choosing things that are going to make you fall asleep certain that you've done at least one thing during the day that you can feel supremely proud of.

(There's also something to be said for that l-word: letting. For *letting* yourself live. For *letting* yourself let go.)

Things are shifting, as sure as the sands in a strong and boisterous wind, and to anyone looking in on my life that has seemingly taken a complete one-eighty shift in the last eight weeks, I certainly look completely and catastrophically crazy.

But there's a method to our collective madness—a madness that means for the first time in years, you can actively choose change and intentionally stack the segments of your life in the exact order you want to create one fluid, flexing, wonderful future. You can play with purpose. You can confidently seduce success, just like you can flirt fearlessly with failure.

The moral of the story?

Don't worry about how your changes make you seem from the outside. Don't worry if your colleagues tease you for your green smoothies. Don't worry if your friend gives you grief for bailing on another happy hour. Don't worry if you haven't quite settled into the silence that happens right before the sun rises. And most importantly, don't worry if everyone doesn't understand.

Because in the perfect words of Cynthia Occelli:

"For a seed to achieve its greatest expression, it must come completely undone. The shell cracks, its insides come out and everything changes. To someone who doesn't understand growth, it would look like complete destruction."

We might break open, spread wide to the wonders of the world and feel so very, very vulnerable. But through those cracks comes a little visceral vine, reaching out into the void, and determined to become something better than it was before.

29

On Having The Biggest Dick In The Room

Hi. I'm Jessica Manuszak, and you may recognize me from such things as that time I talked about shoving in an espresso-soaked tampon, and then again about my confusing wrinkled skin/acne combo, followed up with a hefty dose of shower crying.

And I ~~get stopped in the grocery store~~...~~asked all the time~~...got an email once asking how I managed to land such a sweet gig. Not only do I write all over the dang place, but I'm also the Lead Copywriter, Project Manager and Creative Strategist for a baller and/or shot caller marketing agency. (And no, I never ever get sick of saying that.)

But before I get too into tooting my own horn, (TOOT, TOOT, MOTHERFUCKERS!), I want to tell you a little story.

Once upon a ~~midnight dreary~~ time—

I was on a date with a very debonair gentleman by the name of Trevor, and we were doing the first date thing where he was really into asking me about my job, and I was really into acting like I was really into him, and really not into eating. (Spoiler: Mama loves her cheese. Also, I'm really sorry I just called myself *mama*.)

And while I coyly talked above the rim of my wine glass, red lipstick intact, I regaled the tale of how I spent approximately forever and a day a) cyberstalking my current boss, and b) learning the bare bones of building a website. My plan was to keep studying, keep working, keep improving, and launch a plan of attack when I felt ready.

When the readiness happened, I called in sick to my job in government finance, and put together a website solely for the purpose of getting the woman to hire me. Three weeks later, after toiling over the design and copy (and with the website complete), I typed out a three-sentence email, included the link to the site, took a deep breath, and changed my entire life forever. (<—That's not actually hyperbole, you guys.)

But back to the date.

After my story (during which he laughed and gasped and nodded at all of the appropriate times), my date put down his dessert fork and smiled in a way that made me think I could convince him to let me eat steak off his ass, and simply said—

"You slapped your dick on the table."

I just sort of stared at him, because I didn't know Mr. Investment Banker even knew the word *dick,* let alone went around talking about slapping things with it.

"You slapped your dick on the table," he said again. "And the only people who are confident enough to slap their dick on a table are the people with really good dicks. You're so confident," he said. "You're so brave."

And then I blushed from head to infinity, because apparently I can learn how to sort of build websites, but I still can't figure out how to take a compliment, and HELLO, DID I MENTION HOW ATTRACTIVE HE WAS?!

And then I thought back to the months leading up to me throwing the website at my boss and hoping for the best. How nervous I was. How unsure it was. How my hands were literally shaking when I hit the send button on that one tiny email that let me quit my job dryly crunching numbers and *start actually living.*

My date was totally wrong. I wasn't confident. I sure as hell wasn't brave. But I did a damn good job of acting like I was. And that's the key here—

It's not about having the biggest dick in the room. It's about making people think you do.

So no matter how terrified and uncertain and AHHHHLAKSJELAJSLDJASLDJALURLKASD you feel, just remember that we all feel that way—basically all of the time. But you've got to smooth down your hair, put on your Sunday best, and go after whatever it is that makes your pulse pick up.

And if all else fails? Just stuff some socks down your pants. I hear it totally helps you get *all* the ladies.

30

On Lipstick & Lawns

Fact: I've had more jobs in my life than sexual partners.

I've hopped, skipped, and enthusiastically jumped from one professional position to the next, giving a perfunctory little *toodle-oooh* and going on my merry way. From waitressing to dog washing. From accounting to counting emails. From travel agent to telemarketer.

Because no matter where I was, what I was getting paid, and what I was in charge of, a new job seemed better. Bigger. Brighter. So looking forward to the new and shiny opportunity, I'd abandon ship with a saucy wink and some swing in my step. I was moving UP.

Fact: I've moved apartments more times than I've left the state.

Packed up everything I've owned into huge plastic tubs from Target that I never actually know what to do with once I unpack them. (Spoiler: They get shoved into some unsuspecting closet, taking up space and totally forgotten until the next move.)

Found after hours of perusing Craigslist postings and taking a cursory walk-through, I haul all my shit into a new space with enough natural light to keep me sane, convinced that the NEW apartment is the apartment that will make my confetti-crusted dreams come true.

That the NEW apartment will make me organized. The NEW apartment will coerce me into hosting dinner parties, (and also probably actually cook the dinner for said dinner parties. Doesn't that technology exist yet?!) The NEW apartment will solve all my problems forever and ever, amen. Moving apartments meant moving up.

Fact: I have more red lipsticks in my make-up bag than dollars in my savings account.

Buy a new lipstick. Wear it once. Lose it in the bottom of a purse somewhere never to be seen again (except mayhaps by Jacques Cousteau, what with him being such an accomplished explorer, and all). Despite owning roughly eighty gajillion tubes of almost exactly the same shade of red, each purchase promises the possibility of becoming someone new.

Becoming someone who always remembers to bring reusable grocery bags into the store. Becoming someone who doesn't need to preface a discussion about her BA in poetry by saying,

"It sounds douchey, buuuuuut..." Becoming someone who's laugh is more like a chandelier of champagne glasses and less like Goofy from *A Goofy Movie*. (*Herrr-yuck! Herr-yuck!*)

Buying new lipstick was the answer to all my personal missteps. I was trying to move up.

Fact? All those moves "up" were complete and total bullshit.

Because while improvement is important, so often we get blind-sided by the promise of betterment, convinced that something NEW will make us a NEW PERSON. (Spoiler: New lipstick just makes you the same old you...wearing new lipstick. Who's shocked?)

Instead of throwing out the old, shifting gears, and galloping full-speed ahead to that infamous OTHER SIDE where the grass is (apparently) always greener—

What happens when we post up shop, exactly where we're at, and improve upon things we already have?

Dive in whole-hog at work, taking on new projects that really rev your engine and set your eyes alight,(while pushing you in the right direction of a hefty raise)?

Paint an accent wall steel gray in your loft, spending $42 on burnt orange curtains and adding a damn vanilla-spice Yankee candle?

Commit to one signature shade of red that makes your cheeks

look flushed and your teeth extra white?

I've been around the block enough times to know that staying put isn't always a possibility, but instead of jumping ship and being constantly fueled by that anxious energy that says you HAVE TO WANT MORE, DO MORE, BE MORE, TRY MORE, what happens if we pipe the hell down and cozy up with the lives we've so intentionally built?

Instead of crapping out, running away, and seeking something NEW, let's cultivate contentment and let ourselves live.

After all, the grass isn't greener on the other side. It's greener where you motherfucking water it.

(Bonus: We'll totally get to wear cute gardening gloves, you guys. It's the little things.)

31

On Prison Bitches & Cabana Boys

When I first booked my plane tickets to Costa Rica for a business trip six months ago, I was ecstatic (obviously).

I had very clear visions of deliciously tan cabana boys, bottles of Bacardi, streaming sunshine, and Future Jessica.

The low-down? Future Jessica is someone who has mastered the fine art of wearing white pants without somehow spilling blue Kool-Aid on the crotch (primarily because Future Jessica only drinks mimosas made with champagne and green smoothies).

Future Jessica is able to juggle tiny puggle puppies, invent a language that's an alluring blend of French and German, walk with the perfect sway in her hips, and lets out ladylike laughs that are more gentle tinkling of a wind chime made of wine glasses and less barking outbursts reminiscent of a foghorn.

But when my departure date FINALLY ARRIVED, I woke up with my face glued to my pillow from borderline obscene amounts of drool. I had a new zit on my chin, a deep early morning craving for french fries dipped in hot sauce, and a penchant for sneezing so hard I fart a little.

As I stumbled my way through the Denver airport, shaking cranberry muffin crumbs out of my bra and making overly-long eye contact with any vaguely attractive bearded man (because mother, *may I*?!) I realized that the pristine, perfect, always powered and constantly composed Future Jessica? Has never, and will never exist.

And that's pretty fucking freeing if you think about it.

We'll never be perfectly prepped for international adventures.

We'll never feel totally ready for "monumental" relationship milestones.

We'll never be 100% completely convinced that we can pull off those big business moves.

But you don't have to feel fearless to jump in hairy feet first. (Note: I totally shave my big toe sometimes, just for the record.)

How many times have you bobbled on the brink of something and decided not to go balls deep because you didn't feel ready? Didn't feel capable? Didn't feel like that magical future version of yourself who would be unrelenting ready to go, confidently chomping at the bit and poised to pounce?

(Answer: At least 13.)

Don't shrink away from an exciting endeavor because thinking about it shoves swarms of twitterpated butterflies into your belly. (Though if you barfed, would bugs fly out?! SOMEONE CALL BILL NYE.)

You'll never really be ready.

You'll never be completely convinced you can come out ahead.

You'll never be a rad robot incapable of failure.

But you can always be someone who smacks excuses square on the ass, french kisses fear—assuming fear has a beautiful beard—and dives in (preferably whilst wearing a funny hat).

Stop waiting for the perfect moment.

Instead, make opportunities your prison bitch and decide to be The One Who Did.

32

On Rising From The Ashes Like A Haunted Zombie Mummy Phoenix

(think about it)

Look. The world is a messy place.

It's meticulous in its mayhem, and it's guaranteed that something's going to come around to knock you soundly on your ass, snatch whatever semblance of serenity you had from your outstretched hands, and leave you sprawled out on a dirty street, staring blankly into the gutters, and truly thinking that things can't get any worse.

(Spoiler alert: They can.)

And I'm not saying this to be a discouraging douchemuffin. Or a crap canoe. Or a twatwaffle. Quite the opposite, actually.

Because when life gives you lemons, you have two choices:

Whine like a little shit, or get your shit together.

A or B. Black or white. One or the other.

Because there's no fairy godmother coming to force you into an itchy blue ballgown better suited for that TLC reality show *My Big Fat Gypsy Wedding*. (And don't even get me started on how uncomfortable those damn glass slippers would be. They're heels. MADE OF GLASS.)

No stranger at a bar who's going to lean over, compliment your pity party, and offer you a six-figure salary because you're feeling so certainly sorry for yourself. ("Hi! I've actually been thinking we need a moper on staff. Come aboard the bullshit train! We have oatmeal cookies and lukewarm milk three days past its expiration date!")

No glittery unicorn dust to snort up your nose holes off the back of a badly-lit bathroom toilet seat in a bar somewhere in L.A. that'll make you cry rainbows and poop Twinkies. (Note: Unicorn dust should totally be the new street name for cocaine. You heard it here, first.)

It's not about pulling yourself up by your bootstraps, seeing some anonymous glass finally half-full or looking on the bright side of life.

Because sometimes stuff is the worst.

But just because your circumstances suck, doesn't mean *you* have to.

Just because you want more doesn't mean you have to mope.

And just because you're beaten down doesn't mean you have to get down on yourself.

(Though you're totally welcome to get down with your bad self. Preferably to something with an illicit bass beat.)

You're going to fail. Crash and burn. Get heat rash on the back of your neck, pick at your cuticles until they bleed, and be able to fill plastic milk jugs with your damn tears. (Probably don't try to sell that at yard sales.)

But failing means you're trying, and trying means you're tough. (Like overcooked brisket.)

Your life is not a *Lifetime* original movie. It's a choose your own adventure book. And while there's no *deus ex machina* to step in at the end and ease your struggles, this means you have the final say in how the future turns out.

So, you can't control the cards you're dealt, but you can determine how you deal with them.

Don't stay in the deep holes of whatever the hell pushed you to your knees in the first place. Get the fuck up. Revise, revisit, retry. And become better than you ever believed possible.

33

On Stripping Down

I've spent my entire life running.

(Metaphorically, of course. I haven't started actually running until about four weeks ago, and even then calling it running is being liberal. It's more like shuffling along a dirt path whilst listening to T. Swift at top volume and trying not to swallow the bugs bee-lining for my gaping mouth while I gasp for air. But more on that later.)

From the time I started kindergarten, I knew I wanted to go to college. I worked through school with my head down, taking every AP and honors class I could, cramming extracurriculars into my proverbial basket and crying over a B in advanced calculus (that I got through by counting on my fingers) *because it wasn't an A.*

Quite a few people in my family never graduated high school and opted for their GED instead, but 2007 found me graduating with a GPA of 4.7 (weighted honors classes), wearing those gold ropes that draped down my white robe that said I'd worked hard. That I'd persisted. That I'd never taken my eyes off the future.

Cut to four years later, when I became the first person in my family to graduate college, a BA in Creative Writing under my belt, and 18th in my graduating class of a school with over 40,000 students.

After that, I didn't so much hit the ground running as much as I took off at a sprint, digging my toes in and running wildly towards something. (Fact: I had no idea what I was running to. Or what I was running from. Myself? Myself.)

I needed the money to buy nicer curtains and couches and kitchen appliances for my 400 square-foot studio apartment in the sketchiest part of town so to anyone who came over, it would look like I had my life together (when all I knew for certain was that I didn't know jack shit).

There've been so many jobs and goals and ideas thrown into the mix along the way, until I built the website that got me my current gig, and I've been the absolute happiest clam for almost exactly two years.

But even though I have a cute apartment in a cute part of town, a gorgeous and incredibly compassionate (and hilarious) boyfriend of nine years, and a job that inspires me nearly every single day, I'm still running. Scribbling down to-do lists on fluorescent green post-it notes and sticking them on every available surface, from desktops and corkboards to coffee tables to the toilet seat. (Reminders, after all.)

Find an agent. Get a big book published. Curate every single piece in my apartment. Hike all the 14ers in Colorado this summer. Be the best at painting. Make short films. Start the 7 other blogs I have ideas for. Stick to a strict blog post schedule. Have a huge Twitter following. Grow my TBB Facebook page likes into the tens of thousands. Get more subscribers. Eat nothing but vegetables. Have a million-dollar wardrobe. Travel constantly. Never have my nails unpainted. Clear up my skin. Routinely dye my hair. Get thinner. Get smarter. Get more popular.

My blood pressure spiked just writing that.

And when I think about it, really sit down in the quiet (that as we all know, I've come to dread), I ask myself WHY? Why do I want most of these things? Why do I have that constant hum of anxiety in my stomach urging me to always do more, etching on my insides that it never feels like enough?

Because I care so damn much about how I look to everyone else.

Because I need to be consistently busy, bustling and distracted to feel like I'm doing anything of value. To feel like I am of value.

Would getting a book published be INCREDIBLE? Of course. Duh. Of course it would. But I want it to be the natural result of writing something worth reading. (HI!)

Do I want to spend more time on random creative projects? Yes! But because I enjoy them, not because I want more products to push out into the world.

And do I want to base my feelings of self-worth and success on something as silly as the number of people who like my blog's Facebook page? No. Fuck no. (I actually deleted the page Friday night for just this very reason. That said, do you know it takes 14 days for a page to be finally deleted? I guess to prevent drunk deleting. #themoreyouknow)

I'm stripping out all the noise. Quieting the clutter, and focusing on what I actually want. Novel, right? The things I want because I actually want them for me. Because they bring me joy. Because they fill up my well. Because they're my most personal, personal, PERSONAL wishes that aren't for anyone else's benefit.

I've seen four articles in the last week talking about how stupid and unappealing and damaging to your brand it is to write essays over 500 words (like this one). About content strategy and keywords you need to use in posts to attract more readers. About how important it is to post Facebook ads and promote on Twitter to drive traffic. To boost. Grow. Dominate. Take. Take. Take.

Run.

But what it comes down to—and this might've been the biggest a-ha moment I've had since I first started blogging on LiveJournal at the ripe ol' age of thirteen...

Is that I'm not building a brand. I'm building a life.

And with that comes building in time to just be. To be me. To be brave when the occasion calls for it, but also to roll around in the beauty of the life I have, instead of focusing so hard on the milestones that more often than not, don't actually mean anything to me personally.

As it happens? I'm just lucky enough to have you along with me for the journey.

Group hug? No? Anyone?

34

On Shoving A Square Peg Into A Round Butthole

Success seems to come more easily to some people.

These are the same people who effortlessly wear La Perla lingerie while sprawled out on their bed of money, rolling around in the freshly-pressed dollars and sipping on a dry martini, extra olives.

The same people who somehow don't seem like total elitist assholes when they order that extra shot of espresso in their 14-word morning cup of coffee.

There's an effortlessness to their success.

It seems to roll through 'em like a strong tide, teasing out all their best bits and leaving their minimal flaws in the limelight.

Their email lists boom organically. Their products rake in heaping piles of cash. And their white linen pants—as always—stay pristine & perfect. (Though to be fair, the last bit probably has a fair amount to do with the fact that they probably never eat drippy hamburgers with one hand while careening perilously down the freeway with the windows all the way down and the music all the way up.)

Bitches.

But the only difference between that shiny human being and you? Is that they're capitalizing on that sugary sweet spot where what they're good at and what they're completely obsessed with intersect. (Line graph not included.)

Because if you're not good at something, your business will suffer. And if you don't love something, you'll suffer, too. But when the two collide, potential pours out of every pore, and before you know it, your life will be stuffed with the good stuff.

The bottom line?

Don't try to jam a square peg into a round butthole.

If you're good at numbers but hate math, don't go into government finance. (Trust me—I've done it.) If you love cake decorating but can't make anything that doesn't look like a piping hot pile of baby vomit after a carton of strained peas, it's probably not the best time to open a bakery. If you're good at writing but hate being on camera, don't force yourself to make weekly videos, no matter how en vogue they are.

Trying to cram yourself into a tight little mold that doesn't fit is best described by Cinderella. There she is, in all her flaxen-haired glory, slipping her dainty foot into the dainty slipper and running daintily down the marble steps to her dainty effing future. Daintily.

And then there's the step sister, trying like hell to wedge her flat, fat, sweating foot, (complete with one large wart on the bottom of her big toe), into the delicate balance of glass and glitter. Eventually, the splendid shoe splinters, shattering under the sheer force of being forced where it doesn't belong.

And it's all fun and games until someone gets a handful of glass to the face.

35

On Writing An Essay

1. Pull out a sheet of notebook paper to brainstorm ideas, thinking you've read a bunch of shit about how the visceral connection of putting pen to paper can do wonders for writer's block.

2. Turn on a little Ke$ha to really set the tone for your power-hour idea session.

3. Bop your foot to the tune and begin writing.

4. Realize half an hour later that all you've managed to accomplish is scrawling "Mrs. Joseph Gordon Levitt" 48 times.

5. Check Facebook.

6. Check Twitter.

7. Refresh Facebook

8. Refresh Twitter.

9. Refresh Facebook.

10. Click on a Buzzfeed article.

11. Click on another Buzzfeed article.

12. Lather, rinse, repeat until you've fallen into an internet hole so deep that you've found yourself skimming the one about The Top 20 Male Celebrity Treasure Trails That Resemble Past Presidents or Which 1970's Porn Film Star Is Your Soul Mate? (Spoiler: The answer is always Linda Lovelace.)

13. Drag yourself out of the vortex by your ankles, slamming your laptop shut and trying to compute how many brain cells you've lost.

14. Paint your nails.

15. Four times.

16. In four hours.

17. Contemplate writing a chapter about pick-up lines that would totally work on you, and decide if someone said, "Baby, you must be a fine glass of wine because you have great legs," you'd initiate GO-GO-GADGET NUDITY.

18. Feel the cloud of procrastination hanging over you and melodramatically ruining your life.

19. Pluck your eyebrows in an effort to clear your mind, quickly realizing that having tiny, sparse forehead caterpillars actually makes your eyes look unsettling buggy.

20. Run to Target for sunglasses to hide said buggy eyes.

21. End up buying 3 of the exact same t-shirt in the exact same color because THEY'LL BE SO PRACTICAL WHEN YOU DON'T HAVE TO DO LAUNDRY!

22. Drive home.

23. But take the long way.

24. Clean your kitchen floor.

25. With a toothbrush.

26. Staring at the toothbrush, realize that you sort of have a tooth ache and Google the cause.

27. Deduce you probably have a brain tumor.

28. Call your insurance company's 24/7 nurse's line and start the conversation, "So, Google told me I have a brain tumor..."

29. Think maybe you'll pen a nice letter to a friend, (and somehow end up being the sort of fancypants person who pens letters),

pulling out your stationary and markers.

30. Stare thoughtfully at a brown marker before becoming increasingly curious what you'd look like with a beard.

31. Draw a beard on your face with brown marker.

32. Bask in your innate handsomeness.

33. Hear the doorbell.

34. Realize you've made a terrible mistake.

35. Act nonchalant about your fake facial hair when accepting a package from UPS.

36. Sit cross-legged on the floor and tear open the package, finding a surprise present from a friend.

37. Decide you need to write them a thank you.

38. Stare at the brown marker again.

39. Draw on a fake unibrow.

40. And mutton chops.

41. For good measure.

42. Regret nothing.

43. Decide you need a nickname.

44. Text all your friends, informing them that from now on, they should only refer to you as “The Revolution.”

45. Literally slap yourself across the face, shouting at your empty apartment that you NEED TO GET IT TOGETHER.

46. Pack up all your stuff to head to your favorite coffee shop, thinking a change of scenery will do you some good.

47. Catch your reflection in the mirror and decide you need a shower first.

48. Or maybe a bubble bath.

49. And to shave your legs.

50. And put on lipstick.

51. And straighten your hair.

52. And try on every article of clothing in your closet, even the jeans that are two sizes too small because you’re saving them for that imaginary time when maybe you can suck in enough and hop around to get them zipped.

53. Flex your arm muscles in the mirror.

54. Clean out your closet.

55. Flex your arm muscles in the mirror again.

56. Haul the garbage bags of old clothes out to your car.

57. Donate them to a local shelter.

58. Feel smug as fuck.

59. Go to the coffee shop, but realize it's already the afternoon and all their craft beers are $3.00.

60. Order one beer, just to calm your nerves.

61. Revel in the new-found creativity.

62. Accidentally get day drunk on a Wednesday when you impulsively decide that if one chocolate stout spurs your creativity, four chocolate stouts will make you a damn genius.

63. End up talking to Wilbur, the 78 year-old data analyst, about what it means to find true love.

64. Order a bratwurst wrapped in a pretzel.

65. Think about the small jeans.

66. Dip the bratwurst in queso.

67. Decide you're whatever the opposite of a foodie is.

68. Drip queso on your keyboard.

69. Shamelessly lick it off.

70. Decide the only thing that would go better with the queso is your warm bed.

71. Close down shop.

72. Curtsy on the way out, despite wearing pants.

73. Walk home.

74. Open your laptop.

75. Write a damn essay about it, and hope that it comes off as endearingly self-aware, and not like you're a total asshat incapable of ANY GOOD IDEAS.

36

On Lillian & Catacombs

I've always been comfortable with the feeling of egg yolks rivering down my arms.

Growing up, I lived one block (or exactly 9 houses, the shuttered white one on the corner always giving out king-sized Snickers bars on Halloween) from my Nana's.

Nearly every day in summer, I'd leave our late 1800's buttercup yellow (haunted) Victorian and make the walk, sometimes attempting to expertly maneuver my Skip-It around and around my 7 year-old ankle while crossing the street.

My aunt and I, five years apart, would huddle together on her bedroom floor, our backs against the purple flowered bedspread, gently piercing eggs with thumbtacks on both ends, and blowing out the yolks into empty sour cream containers with the tiny coffee stirring straws we stealthily fisted every time we went to 7-11 for platters of two-dollar nachos and huge blue Slurpees (before jumping on the trampoline and seeing who'd barf first).

And setting those hollowed eggs gingerly on her nightstand, we'd write notes to our future selves, to the future people who'd live at my Nana's, and notes to boys we'd never had the nerve to talk to but sometimes thought about holding hands with at Skate City—rolling them up into tight little bundles and slipping them into their delicate porcelain casings.

Digging through the mountains in her closet, we'd pull out an old jewelry box with Lisa Frank ponies emblazoned across the top, or a teal plastic pencil box, or an old giftbox from her birthday the previous October, dumping out the contents on the carpet and nesting our eggs in thick, wasteful layers of one-ply toilet paper.

Sometimes we'd kiss the eggs with old orange lipstick or sprinkle them gratuitously with huge chunks of multi-colored glitter, but the end result was always the same.

Slipping out the backdoor, walking through the side gate, and hunkering at the base of the lilac bushes in the front yard, the hulking flowers separating my Nana's yard from Lillian's. We'd scrape by the roots with our hands, the dirt caking under our fingernails(all painted a different color), pushing worms out of our way, and jamming the boxes into the ground. Time capsules of our childhood and wishes for future.

Honestly? It was all very cliché , but it made us feel important and romantic. Unique and grown.

And despite our life-or-death levels of secrecy, Lillian would always step out onto her porch seconds after we'd heap dirt over our eggs and pat down the pile, her crooked screen door whining on its hinges and her cane clanking against the worn wood of her porch.

She always called for us, and we always went. Sitting in her tiny living room that was cluttered with the rocks she took from Egypt in 1962, with the poster of her when she was an original pin up model for Coca-Cola, her 16 year-old pincurls immortalized in the painting that sat on the floor. Her big church hats, complete with lace veils that hovered over her left eye with a thin layer of gauze that so perfectly complimented the thin, papery folds of her laugh lines.

She smelled like cold Folger's coffee and dirt roads after it rains, and after laying out a store-bought box of coffee cake and warm black tea, she'd tug the bottom of my curls before settling her 94 year-old ass in a high-backed pink chair and folding her hands into a knot against her soft stomach.

We'd sip our tea, feeling fancy because she always had actual sugar cubes on a tiny plate with silver tongs. She told us about her dead husband, her fingers finding the place on her hand where her ring should be, if it hadn't been stolen in 1978 when they took a trip to Vietnam, three months before he passed. About her time working as a typist in Chicago, where it was inappropriate to show her ankles between the hours of 9 and 5, Monday through Friday. About how much she loved the circus, landing her a midnight date on a San Francisco boardwalk with a fire-breather named Xavier. (Her mother, for the record, did *not* approve.)

And she always reminded us of the same two facts.

"You can either get old, or you can die, and one of those choices means people throw dirt on your face."

And:

"How you spend your days is how you spend your life."

I don't remember the date of Lillian's death. I didn't go to her funeral, and I don't know where she's buried. I don't have a locket with her picture, or a photo of her in a polka-dot bikini, selling bottles of soda from her childhood backyard.

But I remember the way she was always out in her yard as the sun rose, put out plates of canned tuna on tupperware lids for the neighborhood's stray cats, and always patiently watched my aunt and I bury our secrets on her property line.

She lived without apology, a raucous force of adventure that settled next to my Nana long enough to teach me about priorities. To teach me about famous museum heists. To teach me about living life in a way that leaves you worn out and weathered, traveled and well-treated.

She spent her days exhilarated, gaining momentum as she rocketed around the world, setting up shop wherever struck her fancy, finding love and letting it go. She spent her life completely.

We have that opportunity. We have that obligation. To make our days unique pieces of our bigger puzzles, remembering what it means to dig in the dirt and feel uninhibitedly hopeful.

How you spend your days is how you spend your life.

And it's time we all find some fire-breathers, letting them light our way through catacombs and sipping Chardonnay from tea cups.

37

On The 25 New Words You Need To Live Like A Damn Champion

As of late, I've been borderline inappropriately obsessed with making portmanteaus, a super fancy term that basically means cramming two words together to create an entirely new combo word and definition. (They're all over the place. Bootylicious, à la *Destiny's Child*? Booty + delicious. Brainiac? Brain + maniac. Broseidon: King of the Brocean? Bro + Poseidon and bro + ocean.)

With that? BEHOLD.

In alphabetical order, for your convenience.

(Disclaimer: While you won't find these words in the official Merriam-Webster dictionary, you should know that I'm actively resisting calling this a dicktionary and snickering until the cows ~~come home~~ turn up as steak in my dinner.)

Absolucrative *[ab·so·lu·cra·tive] adjective.*
Definition: Used to describe a new business venture that will, undoubtedly, be absolutely lucrative.

Example: "An iPhone for babies?! That's absolucrative!"

Alabastard *[al·a·bas·tard] adjective.*
Definition: When you fall in love with someone who has perfect fair skin like a damn white swan, only to find out they're actually a bastard.

Example: "His blue eyes and pressed Polo were so charming, but after he slept with my best friend on my birthday, I realized he's actually an alabastard."

Aller-Oh-G's *[al·ler·oh·g's] noun.*
Definition: The original gangsters of having the sniffles.

Example: At parties, they're all, "Bitches, please. I had hay fever before that shiz was cool."

Attackle *[at·tack·le] verb.*
Definition: The act of attacking someone via tackle.

Example: "If I ever encounter Joseph Gordon Levitt in person, I'm going to attackle him, and then lick his face in a way that is both charming and super casual."

Bubblebathstrophe *[bub·ble baths·tro·phe] noun.*
Definition: An occurrence when catastrophe strikes in the bubble bath.
Example: "We tried to have a romantic night in, but the soap was aggressively effervescent and it was a total bubblebathstrophe."

Cakeophony *[cake·oph·o·ny] noun.*
Definition: The guttural, offended noise you make the moment after you run out of cake.

Example: "I went to fork in another mouthful of red velvet right as Juan Pablo was giving out his last rose on *The Bachelor*, only to discover that the cake was gone! I totally let out a cakeophony."

Cashtrate *[cash·trate] verb.*
Definition: When all your cash is mercilessly taken away.

Example: "I just finished my Independent Contractor taxes, and the IRS is cashtrating me."

Chinfiltration *[chin·fil·tra·tion] noun.*
Definition: The moment when someone tries to snap a group selfie, and you look at the photo to find that only your chin has made it into the frame.

Example: The person who looks the best in the picture will say things like, "Awhhh! We all look sooooo cute. I love it!" And you'll be like, "Also. My chin."

Grainwashed *[grain·wash·ed] verb; past tense.*
Definition: When you've convinced yourself that you can be one of those women in prescription ads who runs along beaches waving around a ribbon and also has a puppy if only you give up grains and gluten.

Example: "Last night, I found her rocking in a corner, clutching a donut and sobbing. I think she's been grainwashed."

Ginebreation *[gin·e·bri·a·tion] noun.*
Definition: That lovely situation that occurs when you're drunk off gin, and gin alone.

Example: A text you send your friends might read, "Hye ou guys, I lrve gin dna i m soooo ginebriated."

Grindigenous *[grin·dig·e·nous] adjective.*
Definition: A location where grins are BORN.

Example: "You guys, Taco Bell is the most grindigenous place on earth."

Gropeful *[grope·ful] adjective.*
Definition: When someone is hopeful that groping will occur.

Example: "Yeah, I'm going out with Alex today. I'm really gropeful. I'm even wearing my best push-up bra."

Grungeulating *[grun·ge·u·late] verb; present participle.*
Definition: When you're undulating against someone on a dance floor in clothing that pays homage to 90's grunge.

Example: "Man, those singers from Ace of Base are really getting down. They're like the masters of grungeulating."

Indognity *[in·dog·ni·ty] noun.*
Definition: When a dog suffers an indignity.

Example: "My puggle, Brutus, lost his V-card to a panda stuffed animal. OH, THE INDOGNITY."

Kickasserole *[kick·ass·er·ole] noun.*
Definition: When you bake a casserole that kicks an impressive amount of ass.

Example: "Wow, Aunt Judy! These green beans sure made one helluva kickasserole!" (Note: Leave It To Beaver style wholesome smiles not included.)

Naushits *[nau·shits] noun.*
Definition: When you're so sick that stuff is shooting out of both ends, likely thanks to the flu or food poisoning.

Example: "Dude, I totally shouldn't have eaten that steak tartar that was left in my car overnight. I totally have the naushits."

Pumpkinfestation *[pump·kin·fes·ta·tion] noun.*
Definition: That time of year when everything seems to be infested with pumpkin scent and/or flavoring. See also: The

months of September, October, November, and December.

Example: "I'm just drinking my pumpkin spice latte while eating a pumpkin spice Pop Tart and basking in the glow of my pumpkin spice candle and rubbing in pumpkin spice lotion and living in my PUMPKIN SPICE HOUSE. IT'S A PUMPKINFESTATION. SEND HELP."

Resoflutely *[res·o·flute·ly] adverb.*
Definition: When you resolutely complete an action, but punctuate your assertiveness with the charming notes from a flute to lessen the dramatic tension of the moment.

Example: "FINE! I WILL RESOFLUTELY STOP SLASHING YOUR TIRES. *insert charming notes from a flute*"

Sequinfection *[se·quin·fec·tion] noun.*
Definition: Similar to pumpkinfestation (n.), this occurs when you purchase a sequined item that somehow leaves glitter everywhere.

Example: "I just sneezed and my snot came away sparkly. I'm pretty sure I have a sequinfection."

Smassionate *[smas·sion·ate] adjective.*
Definition: When you're so passionate that you smash things in the heat of the moment.

Example: "I mean, she might have broken my great-grandmother's china after I told her about that night in Atlantic City, but it's okay because she's just so smassionate."

Smoothievery *[smoo·thiev·er·y] noun.*
Definition: When some asshole tries to steal your peanut butter and banana smoothie.

Example: "Look, you guys. This is the one day a week I don't have to sneak kale into my breakfast, and there will be NO SMOOTHIEVERY HAPPENING, understand?"

Unicorny *[u·ni·corn·y] adjective.*
Definition: An incredibly cheesy jokes regarding the subject matter of unicorns.

Example: "Hey, I have a unicorny joke. What does a unicorn call its dad? POP CORN!"

Vaginuptials *[va·gi·nup·tials] plural noun.*
Definition: Vows written specifically for a lover's girly bits.

Example: "When I read her my vaginuptials, her down-there area applauded. Metaphorically."

Vitaminimalist *[vi·ta·min·i·mal·ist] noun.*
Definition: Someone who doesn't believe in taking daily multivitamins.

Example: "Susan only licks half a B vitamin every other day. She's a vitaminimalist."

Wienertia *[wie·ner·tia] noun.*
Definition: Because a wiener in motion stays in motion. See also: The rules of inertia.

Example: “He started doing that weird propeller thing with his junk, and it just kept swinging around. It was the first time I’ve seen wienertia first-hand.”

38

On Not Being A Pussy

The thing about me is that I'm a wimp. A scaredy cat. A wuss. (I'm also a redhead, but that feels irrelevant.)

I'm someone who changes lanes on the highway if I end up behind a lumber truck, convinced one of the two-by-fours is going to come unstuck, crashing unceremoniously through my windshield and impaling me thoroughly, gruesome *Final Destination* style.

I step gingerly out of the shower every day, one foot delicately placed on the plush, heather-grey bath mat, and then the other, trying to avoid a slip on the slick porcelain floor of the tub that will surely result in me shattering my skull. (The paramedics would be surprised when they found me, though—the crack in my cranium would probably just be oozing nacho cheese and whiskey gingers.)

And I hate heights. Open-slatted stairs are my greatest enemy, especially the wrought-iron, spiral variety, and after one flight, my ears fill with white noise and my vision blurs. Vertigo. (Luckily, there's no spinning orange vortex à la Alfred Hitchcock.)

But during a business trip to Costa Rica, something snapped. I snapped. And despite every single cell in my body telling me it was a terrible idea, I found myself hauling myself up the wrought-iron, open-slatted stairs of the catamaran onto the top deck, the thigh-high railings doing absolutely nothing to calm my fears.

I was going to jump off the edge. I wanted to be the sort of person who jumped off the edge. I wanted to be the sort of person who wanted to jump off the edge.

And hedging forward, I got in line, watching countless other people pencil-dive into the Pacific, casually stepping off the ledge like they were strolling into the grocery store or crossing the street.

But me? I was making pseudo-joking pleas into a GoPro that should I die, I wanted Mindy Kahling to play me in the made-for-TV movie. I could feel the blood pounding in my ears. And I knew, with absolute certainty, that jumping off the stupid side of that stupid catamaran was going to be one of the hardest things I'd ever done.

There's something to be said for the discomfort that comes with facing your fears. With seeing the possibilities separated in clear-cut black and white. A) I could jump. B) I could climb back down the ladder and go back to being comfortable.

But comfort doesn't catalyze change.

Easy doesn't facilitate success. And doing what you've always done means you'll be who you've always been. (I think we can all agree that stagnation isn't sexy.)

So despite the fact that my legs were so weak I couldn't actually feel them, my pulse had found the rhythm of a hummingbird, and my hands were literally vibrating with fear, I walked to the gap in the railing. I curled my toes over the ledge and watched the gentle lulling of the waves.

But instead of going limp, simply stepping off the side and haphazardly falling, I tensed my thighs.

I gripped hard with my feet. And I grasped the railing on both sides of me tightly, taking one last inhale, and pushing off with everything I had.

Was there an OH SHIT, WHAT HAVE I DONE?! moment before I smacked the water so hard it took my breath away? Absolutely. But I knew—just as surely as I knew there'd be a bruise on my ass from the impact—that by taking a literal, physical and forceful leap, I'd changed a little piece of myself forever.

It's easier to stay where we're at. To stay who we are. To stare unaffected out the window and watch the world fly by.

But we weren't built for biding our time or sitting complacently in back seats. And it's time we not only walk into the unknown, but jump full-throttle into fear, let the briny ocean salt water flood our throats and sting our sinuses, and feel proud that—just for a second—we've proved our past selves completely and totally wrong, putting down that first red brick on a new & noteworthy path.

Epilogue

The year: 3059
(Just kidding. I can't time travel, you guys.)

Samson never wins at bingo.

Every week, I take my rounded bingo marker and stamp a bulbous glob of red ink in his relevant cardboard squares, his vision too blurry and his hands too shaky to do it himself. B-6. G-17. C-1.

And every week, when the bingo cage stops turning and we sit on under-stuffed chairs stamped in faded floral print, Samson and I stare at each other over the rims of our thin Styrofoam cups, the heat from the decaf coffee (all the residents are allowed to have after 4:30 p.m.), making his bifocal glasses fog, the lenses held onto his face by thread-thin wires that tangle behind his ears.

Eventually, he'll start to talk. Usually we talk about his son, one of the original producers of Sesame Street, who won an Emmy and then promptly gave it to his dad. For the record, Samson insists on keeping it on the fireplace mantel in the hobby room so the other residents can enjoy it. Sometimes we talk about Bambi, his late wife who had proudly knitted 4-foot by 4-foot baby blankets for each and every one of their 15 grandchildren. And sometimes we talk about how acidic and weak the coffee is, his crêpe paper face folding up on itself after each and every single bitter sip.

But sometimes, we talk about me.

One day, shifting in his seat, he hoisted his left ankle up onto his right knee, an act that would have seemed casual were it not for the quick grimace that scurried across his face. His socks were tall and black, printed with trains bellowing through thick heaps of steam. I've never wanted a pair of novelty socks so badly in my life.

And leaning forward, he smacked his thin and withered lips and said, "When am I reading your book?" It was more of a statement, than a question, and I took the opportunity to also hoist my left ankle across my right knee, but instead of themed socks, this gave the room a view of the tattoo on my foot–a sweeping arrow that reads *momentum.*

"Eventually," I shrugged. That's all I could really say. I wanted to write a book. Hell, we've all wanted to write books. But I hadn't so much as even opened up a damn Word document to begin.

"That's the thing," he said, separating his trembling hands and tucking them under the sides of his legs to calm the shaking. "I'm going to be dead soon. And I'm not going to give you one single *Get Out of Jail Free* card. When you eventually get around to it, I'll be buried, and you'll feel really guilty. Disappointed, even. And scared that you'll die, too, before you've fixed to make that book come around."

Samson is both a charming and gentle man, but at that very second, I wanted to scream at him so loudly that my spit hit his face. (I didn't, for the record.)

Because he was right, and his words drilled into an exposed nerve, causing a rushed sweep of heat from head to toe and making me feel READY. Before I knew what was happening, I'd promised to get him a manuscript by a date I'd had set in my head for years, but that I'd only finally said out loud for the first time. The numbers felt thick and metallic in my mouth, like coughing up a rusted skeleton key and hoping someone knew where it fit.

And while there's nothing truly profound about setting a date, we've all hedged around direct questions whenever our dreams are brought up.

Circulating at dinner parties, drinking wine the names of which we can't pronounce in dresses that are too tight, people ask us when we'll get engaged and we laugh in a way we think is charming and nonchalant, saying, "Oh, when we get around to it," when we know we're planning to propose in exactly 84 days, sloshing our glasses around and ultimately staining the shiny white grout on their newly-finished kitchen floor.

Sitting around the Thanksgiving table with enough lumpy mashed potatoes on our plates to feed a large thoroughbred horse for a year, our Uncle Richard (the one who always smells like brandy when he tries to kiss us on the lips), asks when we're going to have a talk with our boss about that raise, and we push into our mashed potato mountain until the gravy floods out, drowning the mushy peas that never had any hope of survival, saying, "When I'm good and ready," with a playful wink that we can't pull off. But we already have a meeting to talk about our raise next week.

Or drinking lukewarm, watered-down decaf with a 92 year-old man who mostly remembers our name, but sometimes calls us Jennifer, the name of his girlfriend when he was thirteen, and he asks us when we'll write our book, the book that makes our bodies buzz as we try to fall asleep at night, the words we haven't sat down and stirred up hanging in the air like determined and driven dust. We say, "Eventually," when we *know* when we want to have the project completed.

It's easier to keep our end game a secret. To keep dates and deadlines to ourselves. Because if a silent promise never gets kept, is there a reason to feel ashamed? If a secret goal never gets met, do we fail?

If a tree falls in the forest, does anyone actually give a single, flying fuck?

But as soon as we bellow our beliefs and announce our

ambitions, we're admitting that we're capable of failure. We're cracking ourselves open to scorn. And we're divvying up our dreams for dissection, inviting our friends and family to swarm over our ideas of success and pick through them with knobby and nimble fingers.

But without that dose of drive, that responsibility to hold ourselves accountable and the pride to stand on a wooden crate and shout into a comically large megaphone about exactly what it is we're working for–and when we're going to get it–all we'll be left with is an empty Styrofoam cup, the top rim picked away by our nervous hands.

The sweltering summer sun will dissolve unceremoniously to grey, and we'll spend a solitary drive home through suburbia, thinking about all the incredible people we could possibly be if only we'd let our goals and wants and knowledge be *known*.

So here I sit, at 5:32 p.m. on the last day of my deadline, writing the final sentence of my first real book. Making the tree fall. And sending off the manuscript to man who made me *make*.

Congratulations!

You've officially finished validating Jess' existence. As a reward, please accept 64 SUPER-ROBOT-SHARK points, redeemable for a really, *really* long shower where you can use more shampoo than is fiscally responsible and/or a night of confetti-laden debauchery in an underground discotheque. (The password is *Churro*.)

About the Author

Jessica Manuszak is a rebel with a cause (and also lots of cardigans), standing on the side of a dirt road and annoyingly throwing heaping handfuls of confetti while encouraging you to do whatever the heck it is that makes your pulse race. She'll likely be holding a handmade sign and drinking boxed wine.

Fact: She's endlessly grateful for the top-notch folks at The Frontispiece who made this book look so damn delicious (and reigned in Jess' Oxford Comma addiction).

When she's not trying to sneeze with her eyes open, bidding to win old doorknobs on Ebay, or feeling like a damn CHAMPION on the days she manages to drink the recommended amount of water, you can find her sleeping with the lights on after marathoning shows about ghosts.

She's writing all the damn time at her blog, The Brazen Bible (thebrazenbible.com), where you'll be greeted with a proverbial hug that's so long it'll make you both moderately uncomfortable.

41712596R00119

Made in the USA
Charleston, SC
09 May 2015